A Description of the Cards of the Tarot

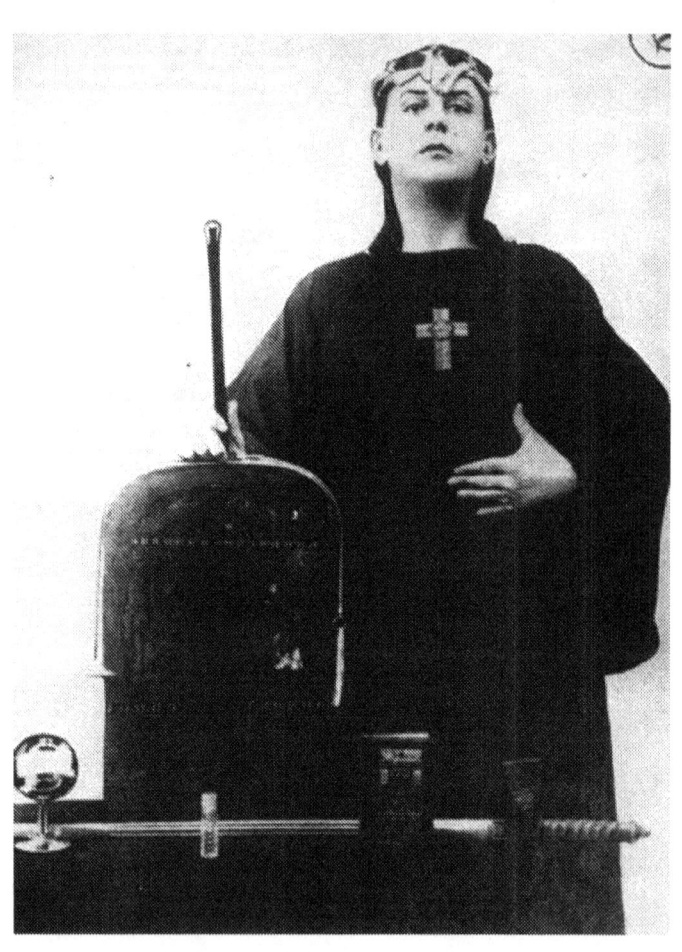

A Description of the Cards of the Tarot

by

Aleister Crowley

THE BOOK TREE
San Diego, California

Originally published
1912
by Weiland & Company
London

New material, revisions and cover
© 2007
The Book Tree
All rights reserved

ISBN 978-1-58509-307-6

Cover layout and design
by Toni Villalas

Published by
The Book Tree
P.O. Box 16476
San Diego, CA 92176
www.thebooktree.com

We provide fascinating and educational products to help awaken the public to new ideas and information that would not be available otherwise.
Call 1 (800) 700-8733 for our *FREE BOOK TREE CATALOG*.

A DESCRIPTION OF
THE CARDS OF THE TAROT
WITH THEIR ATTRIBUTIONS; INCLUDING A
METHOD OF DIVINATION BY THEIR USE

"All divination resembles an attempt by a man born blind to obtain sight by getting blind drunk."

FRA. P.

FOREWORD

This book originally appeared in Crowley's larger volume, The Equinox, in 1912. In is a complete and thorough study of all the cards of the tarot. Each is presented with a detailed description that is highly useful for those who read the cards or want to understand the symbolism better. Includes sections on the thirty-six decans and their relationship to the planets and days of the week, a special chart of the four characteristics of the court cards, how to determine if a card is strong or weak, and reveals a method of divination in the back that is used by Crowley's students. This is a concise handbook recommended to those serious about understanding the tarot.

Paul Tice

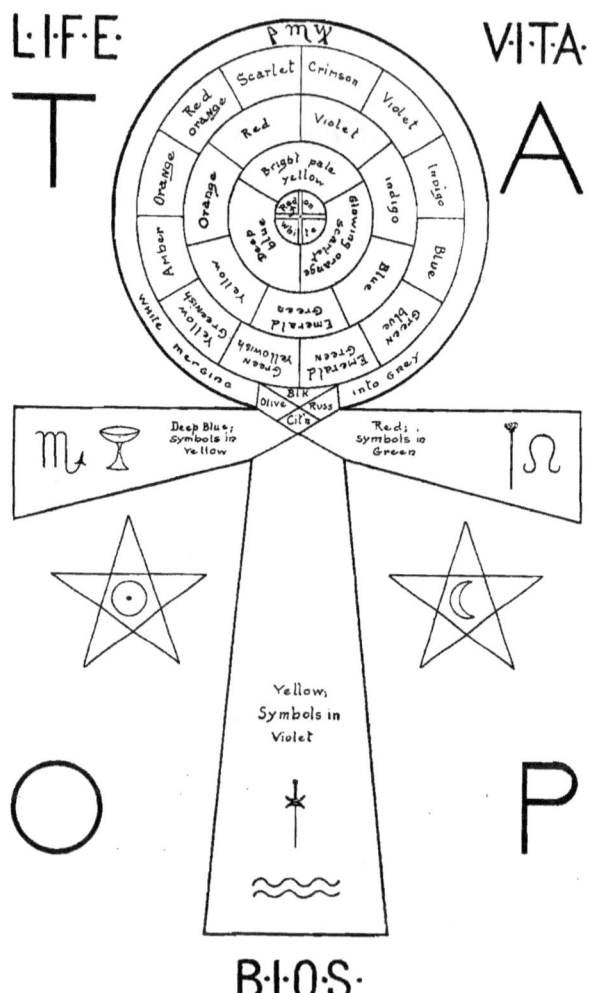

THE COMPLETE SYMBOL OF THE TAROT

A DESCRIPTION OF
THE CARDS OF THE TAROT

H R U
THE GREAT ANGEL
is
set over the operations of the Secret Wisdom

$$A \; καὶ \; \Omega$$

The First and the Last

"WHAT thou seest, write in a book, and send it unto the Seven Abodes which be in Aushiah."

"And I saw in the Right Hand of Him that Sate upon the Throne a Book, sealed with Seven Seals."

"Who is worthy to open the book, and to loose the Seals thereof?"

    S.Y.M.B.O.L.A.

THE FRONTISPIECE

CONSISTS of a Crux Ansata, which is a form of the Rosy Cross. One arm is scarlet, with the symbols of Leo and the Wand in emerald green.

Another is blue with Eagle and Cup in orange.

THE EQUINOX

A third is yellow, with Aquarius and Dagger in violet.

The last is in the four colours of Malkuth, with Pentacle and Taurus in black.

Ring is white, having at the top the Name of the Great Angel P ♏ ♑ H U A; below cross-bar are Pentagrams, one enclosing Sol and the other enclosing Luna.

The whole space in the ring contains the Rose of 22 Petals bearing the Names of the 22 Keys. In the centre a white circle, and a red cross of four equal arms.

About the whole symbol are the words—

      L.I.F.E.   B.I.O.S.   V.I.T.A.,

and the letters—

T. A. P. O., Tarot.

DESCRIPTION OF THE CARDS OF THE TAROT

THE TITLES OF THE SYMBOLS

1. THE Ace of Wands is called the Root of the Powers of Fire.
2. The Ace of Cups is called the Root of the Powers of Water.
3. The Ace of Swords is called the Root of the Powers of Air.
4. The Ace of Pentacles is called the Root of the Powers of Earth.
5. The Knight of Wands is "The Lord of the Flame and Lightning: the King of the Spirits of Fire."
6. The Queen of Wands is "The Queen of the Thrones of Flame."
7. The King of Wands is "The Prince of the Chariot of Fire."
8. The Knave of Wands is "The Princess of the Shining Flame: the Rose of the Palace of Fire."
9. The Knight of Cups is "The Lord of the Waves and the Waters: the King of the Hosts of the Sea."
10. The Queen of Cups is "The Queen of the Thrones of the Waters."
11. The King of Cups is "The Prince of the Chariot of the Waters."
12. The Knave of Cups is "The Princess of the Waters: the Lotus of the Palace of the Floods."

THE EQUINOX

13. The Knight of Swords is "The Lord of the Wind and the Breezes: the King of the Spirits of Air."

14. The Queen of Swords is "The Queen of the Thrones of Air."

15. The King of Swords is "The Prince of the Chariot of the Winds."

16. The Knave of Swords is "The Princess of the Rushing Winds: the Lotus of the Palace of Air."

17. The Knight of Pentacles is "The Lord of the Wide and Fertile Land: the King of the Spirits of Earth."

18. The Queen of Pentacles is "The Queen of the Thrones of Earth."

19. The King of Pentacles is "The Prince of the Chariot of Earth."

20. The Knave of Pentacles is "The Princess of the Echoing Hills: the Rose of the Palace of Earth."

NO.	CARD	LORD OF	DECAN	IN
21.	5 of Wands	Strife	♄	♌
22.	6 ,, ,,	Victory.	♃	♌
23.	7 ,, ,,	Valour.	♂	♌
24.	8 ,, Pentacles	Prudence	☉	♍
25.	9 ,, ,,	Material Gain	♀	♍
26.	10 ,, ,,	Wealth	☿	♍
27.	2 ,, Swords	Peace restored	☽	♎
28.	3 ,, ,,	Sorrow	♄	♎
29.	4 ,, ,,	Rest from Strife	♃	♎
30.	5 ,, Cups	Loss in Pleasure	♂	♍

DESCRIPTION OF THE CARDS OF THE TAROT

NO.	CARD	LORD OF	DECAN	IN
31.	6 ,, ,,	Pleasure	☉	♏
32.	7 ,, ,,	Illusionary Success	♀	♏
33.	8 ,, Wands	Swiftness	☿	♐
34.	9 ,, ,,	Great Strength	☽	♐
35.	10 ,, ,,	Oppression	♄	♐
36.	2 ,, Pentacles	Harmonious Change	♃	♑
37.	3 ,, ,,	Material Works	♂	♑
38.	4 ,, ,,	Earthly Power	☉	♑
39.	5 ,, Swords	Defeat	♀	♒
40.	6 ,, ,,	Earned Success	☿	♒
41.	7 ,, Swords	Unstable Effort	☽	♒
42.	8 ,, Cups	Abandoned Success	♄	♓
43.	9 ,, Cups	Material Happiness	♃	♓
44.	10 ,, ,,	Perfected Success	♂	♓
45.	2 ,, Wands	Dominion	♂	♈
46.	3 ,, ,,	Established Strength	☉	♈
47.	4 ,, ,,	Perfected Work	♀	♈
48.	5 ,, Pentacles	Material Trouble	☿	♉
49.	6 ,, ,,	Material Success	☽	♉
50.	7 ,, ,,	Success unfulfilled	♄	♉
51.	8 ,, Swords	Shortened Force	♃	♊
52.	9 ,, ,,	Despair and Cruelty	♂	♊
53.	10 ,, ,,	Ruin	☉	♊
54.	2 ,, Cups	Love	♀	♋
55.	3 ,, ,,	Abundance	☿	♋
56.	4 ,, ,,	Blended Pleasure	☽	♋

THE EQUINOX

		THE TWENTY-TWO KEYS OF THE BOOK	LETTER	ATTRI-BUTION
57.	0. The Foolish Man	The Spirit of Αἰθήρ	א	A
58.	1. The Magician	The Magus of Power	ב	☿
59.	2. The High Priestess	The Priestess of the Silver Star	ג	☽
60.	3. The Empress	The Daughter of the Mighty Ones	ד	♀
61.	4. The Emperor	Sun of the Morning, chief among the Mighty	ה	♈
62.	5. The Hierophant	The Magus of the Eternal	ו	♉
63.	6. The Lovers	The Children of the Voice; the Oracles of the Mighty Gods	ז	♊
64.	7. The Chariot	The Child of the Powers of the Waters; the Lord of the Triumph of Light	ח	♋
65.	11. Fortitude	The Daughter of the Flaming Sword	ט	♌

DESCRIPTION OF THE CARDS OF THE TAROT

	THE TWENTY-TWO KEYS OF THE BOOK	LETTER	ATTRIBUTION
66. 9. The Hermit.	The Magus of the Voice of Power, the Prophet of the Eternal .	י	♍
67. 10. The Wheel of Fate .	The Lord of the Forces of Life .	כ	♃
68. 8. Justice . .	The Daughter of the Lords of Truth: the Ruler of the Balance .	ל	♎
69. 12. The Hanged Man .	The Spirit of the Mighty Waters . .	מ	▽
70. 13. Death . .	The Child of the Great Transformers: the Lord of the Gates of Death . .	נ	♍
71. 14. Temperance	The Daughter of the Reconcilers: the Bringer-Forth of life .	ס	♐
72. 15. The Devil .	The Lord of the Gates of Matter: the Child of the Forces of Time .	ע	♑

13

THE EQUINOX

	THE TWENTY-TWO KEYS OF THE BOOK	LETTER	ATTRI-BUTION
73. 16. The Blasted Tower .	The Lord of the Hosts of the Mighty . .	פ	♂
74. 17. The Star .	The Daughter of the Firmament, the dweller between the Waters	צ	♒
75. 18. The Moon .	The Ruler of Flux and Reflux: the Child of the Sons of the Mighty . .	ק	♓
76. 19. The Sun .	The Lord of the Fire of the World . .	ר	☉
77. 20. The Judgment .	The Spirit of the Primal Fire .	ש ⊕ and △	
78. 21. The Universe .	The Great One of the Night of Time. . .	ת ▽ and ♄	

Such are the Titles of the
Abodes or Atouts of Thooth;
of the
Mansions of the House of
my
FATHER.

DESCRIPTION OF THE CARDS OF THE TAROT

The Descriptions of the Seventy-eight Symbols
of this Book ⊕ ; together with
their meanings

OF THE ACES

FIRST in order and importance are the Four Aces, representing the Force of the Spirit, acting in, and binding together, the Four Scales of each Element: and answering to the Dominion of the Letters of the Name in the Kether of each. They represent the Radical Forces.

The Four Aces are said to be placed on the North Pole of the Universe wherein they revolve, governing its revolution; and ruling as the connecting link between Yetzirah and the Material Plane or Universe.

I

THE ROOT OF THE POWERS OF FIRE

Ace of Wands

A WHITE Radiating Angelic Hand, issuing from clouds, and grasping a heavy club, which has three branches in the colours, and with the sigils, of the scales. The Right- and Left-hand branches end respectively in three Flames, and the Centre one in four Flames: thus yielding Ten: the Number of the Sephiroth. Two-and-twenty leaping Flames, or Yodh, surround it, answering to the Paths; of these, three fall below the Right branch for Aleph, Mem, and Shin, seven above the Central branch for the double letters; and between it and that on the Right twelve: six above and six below about the Left-hand branch. The whole is a great and flaming Torch. It symbolizes Force—strength, rush, vigour, energy, and it governs, according to its nature, various works and questions.

It implies Natural, as opposed to Invoked, Force.

II

THE ROOT OF THE POWERS OF THE WATERS

Ace of Cups or Chalices

A WHITE Radiant Angelic Hand, issuing from clouds, and supporting on the palm thereof a cup, resembling that of the Stolistes.

From it rises a fountain of clear and glistening water: and sprays falling on all sides into clear calm water below, in which grow Lotuses and Water-lilies. The great Letter of the Supernal Mother is traced in the spray of the Fountain.

It symbolizes Fertility—productiveness, beauty, pleasure, happiness, etc.

DESCRIPTION OF THE CARDS OF THE TAROT

III

THE ROOT OF THE POWERS OF THE AIR

Ace of Swords

A WHITE Radiating Angelic Hand, issuing from clouds, and grasping the hilt of a sword, which supports a White Radiant Celestial Crown; from which depend, on the right, the olive branch of Peace; and on the left, the palm branch of suffering.

Six Vaus fall from its point. It symbolizes *Invoked*, as contrasted with Natural Force: for it is the Invocation of the Sword. Raised upward, it invokes the Divine crown of Spiritual Brightness, but reversed it is the Invocation of Demonic Force; and becomes a fearfully evil symbol. It represents, therefore, very great power for good or evil, but invoked; and it also represents whirling Force, and strength through trouble. It is the affirmation of Justice upholding Divine Authority; and it may become the Sword of Wrath, Punishment, and Affliction.

IV

THE ROOT OF THE POWERS OF THE EARTH

Ace of Pentacles

A WHITE Radiant Angelic Hand, holding a branch of a Rose Tree, whereon is a large Pentacle, formed of Five concentric circles. The Innermost Circle is white, charged with

THE EQUINOX

a red Greek Cross. From this White Centre, Twelve Rays, also white, issue: these terminate at the circumference, making the whole something like an Astrological figure of the Heavens.

It is surmounted by a small circle, above which is a large white Maltese Cross, and with two white wings.

Four Crosses and two buds are shewn. The Hand issueth from the Clouds as in the other three cases.

It represents materiality in all senses, good and evil: and is, therefore, in a sense, illusionary: it shows material gain, labour, power, wealth, etc.

THE SIXTEEN COURT, OR ROYAL CARDS

The Four Kings

THE Four Kings, or "Figures mounted on steeds," represent the Yodh forces of the Name in each Suit: the Radix, Father and commencement of Material Forces, a force in which all the others are implied, and of which they form the development and completion. A force swift and violent in its action, but whose effect soon passes away, and therefore symbolized by a Figure on a Steed riding swiftly, and clothed in complete Armour.

Therefore is the knowledge of the scale of the King so necessary for the commencement of all magical working.

DESCRIPTION OF THE CARDS OF THE TAROT

The Four Queens

are seated upon Thrones; representing the Forces of the Hé of the Name in each suit; the Mother and bringer-forth of Material Forces: a force which develops and realizes that of the King: a force steady and unshaken, but not rapid, though enduring. It is therefore symbolized by a Figure seated upon a Throne: but also clothed in Armour.

The Four Princes

These Princes are Figures seated in Chariots, and thus borne forward. They represent the Vau Forces of the Name in each suit: the Mighty Son of the King and Queen, who realizes the influence of both scales of Force. A Prince, the son of a King and Queen, yet a Prince of Princes, and a King of Kings: an Emperor whose effect is at once rapid (though not so swift as that of the Queen) and enduring. It is, therefore, symbolized by a Figure borne in a Chariot, and clothed in Armour. Yet is his power vain and illusionary, unless set in Motion by his Father and Mother.

The Four Princesses

are the Knaves of the Tarot Pack; The Four Princesses or figures of Amazons, standing firmly of themselves: neither riding upon Horses, nor seated upon Thrones, nor borne in

Chariots. They represent the forces of the Hé final of the Name in each suit, completing the Influences of the other scales: The mighty and potent daughter of a King and Queen: a Princess powerful and terrible: a Queen of Queens—an Empress—whose effect combines those of the King, Queen, and Prince, at once violent and permanent; therefore symbolized by a Figure standing firmly by itself, only partially draped, and having but little Armour; yet her power existeth not, save by reason of the others: and then indeed it is mighty and terrible materially, and is the Throne of the Forces of the Spirit.

Woe unto whomsoever shall make war upon her, when thus established!

THE SPHERES OF INFLUENCE OF THE COURT CARDS OF THE TAROT PACK

THE Princesses rule the Four Parts of the Celestial Heavens which lie around the North Pole, and above the respective Cherubic Signs of the Zodiac, and they form the Thrones of the Powers of the Four Aces.

The twelve cards, the Four Kings, Queens and Princes rule the dominion of the Celestial Heavens, between the realm of the Four Princesses and the Zodiac, as is hereafter shewn. And they, as it were, link together the signs.

DESCRIPTION OF THE CARDS OF THE TAROT

V

THE LORD OF THE FLAME AND THE LIGHTNING; THE KING OF THE SPIRITS OF FIRE

Knight[1] of Wands

A WINGED Warrior riding upon a black horse with flaming mane and tail: the horse itself is not winged. The rider wears a winged helmet (like the old Scandinavian and Gaulish helmet) with a Rayed Crown, a corslet of scale-mail and buskins of the same, and a flowing scarlet mantle. Above his helmet, upon his cuirass, and on the shoulder-pieces and buskins, he wears as a crest a winged black horse's head. He grasps a club with flaming ends, somewhat similar to that in the symbol of the Ace of Wands, but not so heavy, and also the sigil of his scale is shown; beneath the rushing feet of his steed are waving flames and fire. He is active—generous—fierce—sudden—impetuous.

If ill dignified, he is evil-minded—cruel—bigoted—brutal. He rules the celestial heavens from above the Twentieth Degree of ♍ to the First Two Decans of ♐ : and this includes a part of the Constellation Hercules. (Hercules is always represented with a Club.)

△ of △
King of the Salamanders.

---

[1] Note that the Kings are now called Knights, and the Princes are now called Kings. This is unfortunate, and leads to confusion; the Princes may be called Emperors without harm. Remember only that the horsed figures refer to the Yod of Tetragrammaton, the charioted figures to the Vau.

THE EQUINOX

VI

THE QUEEN OF THE THRONES OF FLAME

Queen of Wands

A CROWNED Queen with long red-golden hair, seated upon a Throne, with steady flames beneath. She wears a corslet and buskins of scale-mail, which latter her robe discloses. Her arms are almost bare. On cuirass and buskins are leopard's heads winged, and the same symbol surmounteth her crown. At her side is a couchant leopard on which her hands rest. She bears a long wand with a very heavy conical head. The face is beautiful and resolute.

Adaptability, steady force applied to an object, steady rule, great attractive power, power of command, yet liked notwithstanding. Kind and generous when not opposed.

If ill dignified, obstinate, revengeful, domineering, tyrannical, and apt to turn against another without a cause.

She rules the heavens from above the last Decan of ♓ to above the 20° of Aries : including thus a part of Andromeda.

▽. of △
Queen of the Salamanders.

VII

THE PRINCE OF THE CHARIOT OF FIRE

King of Wands

A KINGLY Figure with a golden, winged crown, seated on a chariot. He has large white wings. One wheel of his chariot

DESCRIPTION OF THE CARDS OF THE TAROT

is shewn. He wears corslet and buskins of scale armour decorated with a winged lion's head, which symbol also surmounts his crown. His chariot is drawn by a lion. His arms are bare, save for the shoulder-pieces of the corslet, and he bears a torch or fire-wand, somewhat similar to that of the Zelator Adeptus Minor. Beneath the chariot are flames, some waved, some salient.

Swift, strong, hasty; rather violent, yet just and generous; noble and scorning meanness.

If ill dignified—cruel, intolerant, prejudiced and ill natured.

He rules the heavens from above the last Decan of ♋ to the second Decan of Leo; hence he includes most of Leo Minor.

△ of △
Prince and Emperor of Salamanders.

VIII

THE PRINCESS OF THE SHINING FLAME; THE ROSE OF THE PALACE OF FIRE

Knave of Wands

A VERY strong and beautiful woman with flowing red-gold hair, attired like an Amazon. Her shoulders, arms, bosom and knees are bare. She wears a short kilt reaching to the knee. Round her waist is a broad belt of scale-mail; narrow at the sides; broader in front and back; and having a winged tiger's head in front. She wears a Corinthian-shaped helmet and crown with a long plume. It also is surmounted by a tiger's head, and the same symbol forms the buckle of her scale-mail buskins. A mantle lined with tiger's skin falls back from her shoulders. Her right hand rests on a small golden or brazen altar ornamented with rams' heads and with Flames of Fire leaping from it. Her left hand leans on a long and heavy club, swelling at the lower end, where the sigil is placed; and it has flames of fire leaping from it the whole way down; but the flames are ascending. This club or torch is much longer than that carried by the King or Queen. Beneath her firmly placed feet are leaping Flames of Fire.

Brilliance, courage, beauty, force, sudden in anger or love, desire of power, enthusiasm, revenge.

If ill dignified, she is superficial, theatrical, cruel, unstable, domineering.

She rules the heavens over one quadrant of the portion around the North Pole.

∇ of △
Princess and Empress of the Salamanders.
Throne of the Ace of Wands.

IX

THE LORD OF THE WAVES AND THE WATERS; THE KING OF THE HOSTS OF THE SEA

Knight of Cups

A BEAUTIFUL, winged, youthful Warrior with flying hair, riding upon a white horse, which latter is not winged. His general equipment is similar to that of the Knight of Wands,

DESCRIPTION OF THE CARDS OF THE TAROT

but upon his helmet, cuirass and buskins is a peacock with opened wings. He holds a cup in his hand, bearing the sigil of the scale. Beneath his horse's feet is the sea. From the cup issues a crab.

Graceful, poetic, Venusian, indolent, but enthusiastic if roused.

Ill dignified, he is sensual, idle and untruthful.

He rules the heavens from above 20° of ♒ to 20° of ♓, thus including the greater part of Pegasus.

△ of ▽.
King of Undines and Nymphs.

X

THE QUEEN OF THE THRONES OF THE WATERS

Queen of Cups

A VERY beautiful fair woman like a crowned Queen, seated upon a throne, beneath which is flowing water wherein Lotuses are seen. Her general dress is similar to that of the Queen of Wands, but upon her crown, cuirass and buskins is seen an Ibis with opened wings, and beside her is the same bird, whereon her hand rests. She holds a cup, wherefrom a crayfish issues. Her face is dreamy. She holds a lotus in the hand upon the Ibis.

She is imaginative, poetic, kind, yet not willing to take much trouble for another. Coquettish, good-natured underneath a dreamy appearance. Imagination stronger than

THE EQUINOX

feeling. Very much affected by other influences, and therefore more dependent upon dignity than most symbols.

She rules from 20° ♊ to 20° ♋.

▽ of ▽
Queen of Nymphs or Undines.

XI

THE PRINCE OF THE CHARIOT OF THE WATERS

King of Cups

A WINGED Kingly Figure with winged crown seated in a chariot drawn by an eagle. On the wheel is the symbol of a scorpion. The eagle is borne as a crest on his crown, cuirass and buskins. General attire like King of Wands. Beneath his chariot is the calm and stagnant water of a lake. His armour resembles feathers more than scales. He holds in one hand a lotus, and in the other a cup, charged with the sigil of his scale. A serpent issues from the cup, and has its head tending down to the waters of the lake. He is subtle, violent, crafty and artistic; a fierce nature with calm exterior. Powerful for good or evil, but more attracted by the evil if allied with apparent Power or Wisdom.

If ill dignified, he is intensely evil and merciless.

He rules from 20° ♎ to 20° ♏.

△ of ▽
Prince and Emperor of Nymphs or Undines.

DESCRIPTION OF THE CARDS OF THE TAROT

XII

THE PRINCESS OF THE WATERS; THE LOTUS OF THE PALACE OF THE FLOODS

Knave of Cups

A BEAUTIFUL Amazon-like figure, softer in nature than the Princess of Wands. Her attire is similar. She stands on a sea with foaming spray. Away to her right a Dolphin. She wears as a crest a swan with opening wings. She bears in one hand a lotus, and in the other an open cup from which a turtle issues. Her mantle is lined with swansdown, and is of thin floating material.

Sweetness, poetry, gentleness and kindness. Imaginative, dreamy, at times indolent, yet courageous if roused.

When ill dignified she is selfish and luxurious.

She rules a quadrant of the heavens around Kether.

∀ of ∇
Princess and Empress of the Nymphs or Undines
Throne of the Ace of Cups.

XIII

THE LORD OF THE WINDS AND THE BREEZES: THE KING OF THE SPIRITS OF AIR

Knight of Swords

A WINGED Warrior with crowned Winged Helmet, mounted upon a brown steed. His general equipment is

THE EQUINOX

as that of the Knight of Wands, but he wears as a crest a winged six-pointed star, similar to those represented on the heads of Castor and Pollux the Dioscuri, the twins Gemini (a part of which constellation is included in his rule). He holds a drawn sword with the sigil of his scale upon its pommel. Beneath his horse's feet are dark-driving stratus clouds.

He is active, clever, subtle, fierce, delicate, courageous, skilful, but inclined to domineer. Also to overvalue small things, unless well dignified.

If ill dignified, deceitful, tyrannical and crafty.

Rules from 20° ♉ to 20° ♊.

△ of ♎
King of the Sylphs and Sylphides.

XIV

THE QUEEN OF THE THRONES OF AIR

Queen of Swords

A GRACEFUL woman with wavy, curling hair, like a Queen seated upon a Throne and crowned. Beneath the Throne are grey cumulus clouds. Her general attire is as that of the Queen of Wands, but she wears as a crest a winged child's head. A drawn sword in one hand, and in the other a large, bearded, newly severed head of a man.

Intensely perceptive, keen observation, subtle, quick and confident: often persevering, accurate in superficial things, graceful, fond of dancing and balancing.

DESCRIPTION OF THE CARDS OF THE TAROT

If ill dignified, cruel, sly, deceitful, unreliable, though with a good exterior.

Rules from 20° ♏ to 20° ♎.

▽ of △

Queen of the Sylphs and Sylphides.

XV
THE PRINCE OF THE CHARIOT OF THE WINDS

King of Swords

A WINGED King with Winged Crown, seated in a chariot drawn by Arch Fays, represented as winged youths very slightly dressed, with butterfly wings: heads encircled by a fillet with a pentagram thereon: and holding wands surmounted by pentagrams, the same butterfly wings on their feet and fillets. General equipment as the King of Wands: but he bears as a crest a winged angelic head with a pentagram on the brows. Beneath the chariot are grey nimbus clouds. His hair long and waving in serpentine whirls, and whorl figures compose the scales of his armour. A drawn sword in one hand; a sickle in the other. With the sword he rules, with the sickle he slays.

Full of ideas and thoughts and designs, distrustful, suspicious, firm in friendship and enmity; careful, observant, slow, over-cautious, symbolizes △ and ♌; he slays as fast as he creates.

THE EQUINOX

If ill dignified: harsh, malicious, plotting; obstinate, yet hesitating; unreliable.

Rules from 20° ♑ to 20° ♒.

△ of △
Prince and Emperor of Sylphs and Sylphides.

XVI

THE PRINCESS OF THE RUSHING WINDS: THE LOTUS OF THE PALACE OF AIR

Knave of Swords

AN AMAZON figure with waving hair, slighter than the Rose of the Palace of Fire. Her attire is similar. The Feet seem springy, giving the idea of swiftness. Weight changing from one foot to another and body swinging around. She is a mixture of Minerva and Diana: her mantle resembles the Ægis of Minerva. She wears as a crest the head of the Medusa with serpent hair. She holds a sword in one hand; and the other rests upon a small silver altar with grey smoke (no fire) ascending from it. Beneath her feet are white clouds.

Wisdom, strength, acuteness; subtlety in material things: grace and dexterity.

If ill dignified, she is frivolous and cunning.

She rules a quadrant of the heavens around Kether.

▽ of △
Princess and Empress of the Sylphs and Sylphides.
Throne of the Ace of Wands.

DESCRIPTION OF THE CARDS OF THE TAROT

XVII

THE LORD OF THE WIDE AND FERTILE LAND;
THE KING OF THE SPIRITS OF EARTH

Knight of Pentacles

A DARK Winged Warrior with winged and crowned helmet: mounted on a light brown horse. Equipment as the Knight of Wands.

The winged head of a stag or antelope as a crest. Beneath the horse's feet is fertile land with ripened corn. In one hand he bears a sceptre surmounted by a hexagram: in the other a Pentacle like that of the Zelator Adeptus Minor.

Unless very well dignified he is heavy, dull, and material. Laborious, clever, and patient in material matters.

If ill dignified, he is avaricious, grasping, dull, jealous; not very courageous, unless assisted by other symbols.

Rules from above 20° of ♌ to 20° of ♍.

△ of ▽
King of Gnomes.

XVIII

THE QUEEN OF THE THRONES OF EARTH

Queen of Pentacles

A WOMAN of beautiful face with dark hair; seated upon a throne, beneath which is dark sandy earth. One side of her face is light, the other dark; and her symbolism is best

THE EQUINOX

represented in profile. Her attire is similar to that of the Queen of Wands: but she bears a winged goat's head as a crest. A goat is by her side. In one hand she bears a sceptre surmounted by a cube, and in the other an orb of gold.

She is impetuous, kind; timid, rather charming; greathearted; intelligent, melancholy; truthful, yet of many moods.

If ill dignified she is undecided, capricious, changeable, foolish.

She rules from 20° ♐ to 20° ♍.

▽ of ▽
The Queen of Gnomes.

XIX

THE PRINCE OF THE CHARIOT OF EARTH

King of Pentacles

A WINGED Kingly Figure seated in a chariot drawn by a bull. He bears as a crest the symbol of the head of the winged bull. Beneath the chariot is land, with many flowers. In one hand he bears an orb of gold held downwards, and in the other a sceptre surmounted by an orb and cross.

Increase of matter. Increases good or evil, solidifies; practically applies things. Steady; reliable.

If ill dignified he is selfish, animal and material: stupid. In either case slow to anger, but furious if roused.

DESCRIPTION OF THE CARDS OF THE TAROT

Rules from 20° ♈ to 20° ♉.

△ of ▽
Prince and Emperor of the Gnomes.

XX

PRINCESS OF THE ECHOING HILLS: ROSE OF THE PALACE OF EARTH

Knave of Pentacles

A STRONG and beautiful Amazon figure with rich brown hair, standing on grass or flowers. A grove of trees near her. Her form suggests Hebe, Ceres, and Proserpine. She bears a winged ram's head as a crest: and wears a mantle of sheepskin. In one hand she carries a sceptre with a circular disk: in the other a Pentacle similar to that of the Ace of Pentacles.

She is generous, kind, diligent, benevolent, careful, courageous, persevering, pitiful.

If ill dignified she is wasteful and prodigal. She rules over one quadrant of the heavens around the North Pole of the Ecliptic.

▽ of ▽
Princess and Empress of the Gnomes.
Throne of the Ace of Pentacles.

THE EQUINOX

HEREIN ARE RESUMED THE ESPECIAL CHARACTERISTICS OF THE FOUR COURT CARDS OF THE SUITS

SUITS	CARDS	CRESTS	SYMBOLS	HAIR	EYES
WANDS	King	Winged black horse's head	Black horse, waving flames, club, scarlet cloak	Red-gold	Grey or hazel
	Queen	Leopard's head, winged	Leopard, steady flames, wand with heavy head or end	Red-gold	Blue or brown
	Prince	Lion's head, winged	Waved and salient flames, fire wand of Zelator Adept	Yellow	Blue-grey
	Princess	Tiger's head	Tiger, leaping flames, gold altar, long club, largest at bottom	Red-gold	Blue
CUPS	King	Peacock with opened fan	White horse, crab issuing from cup, sea	Fair	Blue
	Queen	Ibis	Ibis, crayfish issuing from cup, river	Gold-brown	Blue
	Prince	Eagle	Scorpion, eagle; serpent issuing from cup, lake	Brown	Grey or brown
	Princess	Swan	Dolphin lotus, sea with spray, turtle from cup	Brown	Blue or brown
SWORDS	King	Winged hexagram	Winged brown horse, driving clouds, drawn sword	Dark-brown	Dark
	Queen	Winged child's head	Head of man severed, cumulus clouds, drawn sword	Light-brown	Grey
	Prince	Winged Angel's head	Arch fairies winged, whirling hair, nimbi, drawn sword and sickle	Dark	Dark
	Princess	Medusa's head	Silver altar, smoke, clouds, drawn sword	Light-brown	Blue
PENTACLES	King	Winged stag's head	Light-brown horse, ripe cornland, sceptre with hexagram, pentacle as Zelator Adept.	Dark	Dark
	Queen	Winged goat's head	Barren land, fan, light one side only, sceptre with cube, orb of gold	Dark	Dark
	Prince	Winged bull's head	Flowery land, bull, sceptre with orb and cross, orb held downwards	Dark-brown	Dark
	Princess	Winged ram's head	Grass, flowers, grove of trees, sceptre with disk, pentacle like that in ace	Rich brown	Dark

DESCRIPTION OF THE CARDS OF THE TAROT

OF THE THIRTY-SIX DECANS

HERE follow the descriptions of the smaller cards of the four suits, thirty-six in number, answering unto the thirty-six Decans of the Zodiac.

Commencing from the sign Aries, the *Central* Decans of each sign follow the order of the Days of the Week. Thus—

CARD	CENTRAL DECAN OF	MEANING	DAY
3 of Wands	♈	Established Strength	☉
6 ,, P.	♉	Material Success	☽
9 ,, S.	♊	Despair and Cruelty	♂
3 ,, C.	♋	Abundance	☿
6 ,, W.	♌	Victory	♃
9 ,, P.	♍	Material Gain	♀
3 ,, S.	♎	Sorrow	♄
6 ,, C.	♏	Pleasure	☉
9 ,, W.	♐	Great Strength	☽
3 ,, P.	♑	Material Works	♂
6 ,, S.	♒	Earned Success	☿
9 ,, C.	♓	Material Happiness	♃

Being thus the Four Threes, Sixes, and Nines.

The first and third Decans follow the same order: Sunday beginning in the First Decan of ♍ and in the Third Decans of ♊ and ♑.

THE EQUINOX

The planets govern respectively Decans with the following Titles—

♄

1.	♌	Strife	5 of Wands.
2.	♎	Sorrow	3 ,, Swords.
3.	♐	Oppression	10 ,, Wands.
4.	♓	Abundant Success	8 ,, Cups.
5.	♉	Success Unfulfilled	7 ,, Pentacles.

Or in ♉ ♌ ♎ ♐ ♓ two wands : 1 each of the other suits.

♃

1.	♌	Victory	6 of Wands.
2.	♎	Rest from Strife	4 ,, Swords.
3.	♑	Harmonious Change	2 ,, Pentacles.
4.	♓	Material Happiness	9 ,, Cups.
5.	♊	Shortened Force	8 ,, Swords.

Or in ♊ ♌ ♎ ♑ ♓ two swords : 1 each of others.

♂

1.	♌	Valour	7 of Wands.
2.	♏	Loss in Pleasure	5 ,, Cups.
3.	♑	Material Works	3 ,, Pentacles.
4.	♓	Perfected Success	10 ,, Cups.
5.	♈	Dominion	2 ,, Wands.
6.	♊	Despair and Cruelty	9 ,, Swords.

Or in ♈ ♊ ♌ ♏ ♑ ♓ 2 W. 2 C. : 1 each of others.

One more Decan than the others.

☉

| 1. | ♍ | Prudence | 8 of Pentacles. |
| 2. | ♏ | Pleasure | 6 ,, Cups. |

DESCRIPTION OF THE CARDS OF THE TAROT

3.	♑	Earthly Power	4 of Pentacles.
4.	♈	Established Strength	3 ,, Wands.
5.	♊	Ruin	10 ,, Swords.

Or in ♈ ♊ ♍ ♏ ♑ 2 pentacles : 1 each of others.

♀

1.	♍	Material Gain	9 of Pentacles.
2.	♏	Illusionary Success	7 ,, Cups.
3.	♒	Defeat	5 ,, Swords.
4.	♈	Perfected Work	4 ,, Wands.
5.	♋	Love	2 ,, Cups.

Or in ♈ ♋ ♍ ♏ ♒ 2 Cups : 1 each of others.

☿

1.	♍	Wealth	10 of Pentacles.
2.	♐	Swiftness	8 ,, Wands.
3.	♒	Earned Success	6 ,, Swords.
4.	♉	Material Trouble	5 ,, Pentacles.
5.	♋	Abundance	3 ,, Cups.

Or in ♉ ♋ ♍ ♐ ♒ two Pentacles : 1 of each of the others.

☽

1.	♎	Peace Restored	2 of Swords.
2.	♐	Great Strength	9 ,, Wands.
3.	♒	Unstable Effort	7 ,, Swords.
4.	♉	Material Success	6 ,, Pentacles.
5.	♋	Blended Pleasure	4 ,, Cups.

Or in ♉ ♋ ♎ ♐ ♒ two Swords : 1 of each of the others.

There being thirty-six Decans and seven Planets, it follows that one of the latter must rule over one more Decan than the others. This is the Planet Mars, to which are allotted the last Decan of ♓, and the first of ♈, because the long cold of the winter requires a great energy to overcome it, and initiate spring.

And the beginning of the Decanates is from the royal Star of Leo, the great Star Cor Leonis: and therefore is the first Decan that of ל in ♉.

Here follow the general meanings of the small cards of the suits, as classified under the nine Sephiroth below Kether.

חכמה The Four Twos symbolize the Powers of the King and Queen just uniting and initiating the Force; but before the Prince and Princess are thoroughly brought into action. Therefore do they generally imply the initiation and fecundation of a thing.

בינה Realization of action owing to the Prince being produced. The central symbol on each card. Action definitely commenced for good or evil.

חסד Perfection, realization, completion: making a matter settled and fixed.

גבורה Opposition, strife and struggle: war; obstacle to the thing in hand. Ultimate success or failure is otherwise shewn.

תפארת Definite accomplishment. Thing carried out.

נצח Generally shew a force transcending the Material Plane: and is like unto a Crown; which, indeed, is powerful, but requireth one capable of wearing it. The Sevens then shew a possible result: which is dependent on the action then taken. They depend much on the symbols that accompany them.

DESCRIPTION OF THE CARDS OF THE TAROT

הוד Solitary success: *i.e.* success in the matter for the time being: but not leading to much result apart from the thing itself.

יסוד Very great fundamental force. Executive power, because they restore a firm basis. Powerful for good or evil.

מלכות Fixed, culminated, complete Force, whether good or evil. The matter thoroughly and definitely determined. Ultimating Force.

Follow the particular descriptions of each of the thirty-six cards: with full meanings.

Decan-cards are always modified by the other symbols with which they are in contact.

XXI

THE LORD OF STRIFE

Five of Wands

Two White Radiant Angelic Hands issuant per nubes dexter and sinister. They are clasped together in the grip of the First Order, *i.e.* the four fingers of each right hand crooked into each other, the thumbs meeting above; and they hold, at the same time, by their centres, five wands or torches which are similar unto the wands of a Zelator Adeptus Minor. One wand is upright in the middle; the others cross each other. Flames leap from the point of junction. Above the middle wand is the sign ♄, and below is that of ♌ : thus representing the Decanate. Violent strife and boldness, rashness, cruelty, violence, lust, desire, prodigality and generosity ; depending on whether the card is well or ill dignified.

THE EQUINOX

Geburah of ' (Quarrelling and fighting).

This Decan hath its beginning from the Royal Star of Leo: and unto it are allotted the two great Angels of the Schemhamphorash והויה and יליאל.

[The proper meaning of the small cards is to be found by making thorough meditation and harmony between these four symbols of each card. It will be seen that this is how the meanings have been done; but the advanced student can go beyond this rude working.]

XXII

THE LORD OF VICTORY

Six of Wands

Two hands in grip as the last, holding six wands crossed three and three. Flames issue from the point of junction. Above and below are short wands with flames issuing, surmounted respectively by the symbols of ♃ and ♌, representing the Decan.

Victory after strife: Love: pleasure gained by labour: carefulness, sociability and avoiding of strife, yet victory therein: also insolence, and pride of riches and success, etc. The whole dependent on the dignity.

Tiphareth of ' (Gain).

Hereunto are allotted the great Angels סיטאל and עלמיה of the Schemhamphorash.

DESCRIPTION OF THE CARDS OF THE TAROT

XXIII

THE LORD OF VALOUR

Seven of Wands

Two hands holding by grip six wands, three crossed. A third hand issuing from a cloud at the lower part of the card, holding an upright wand which passes between the others. Flames leap from the point of junction. Above and below the central wand are the symbols of Mars and Leo, representing the Decan.

Possible victory, depending on the energy and courage exercised; valour; opposition, obstacles and difficulties, yet courage to meet them; quarrelling, ignorance, pretence, and wrangling, and threatening; also victory in small and unimportant things: and influence upon subordinates.

Netzach of ♦ (Opposition, yet courage).

Therein rule the two great Angels מהשיה and ללהאל of the Schemhamphorash.

XXIV

THE LORD OF PRUDENCE

Eight of Pentacles

A WHITE Radiating Angelic Hand, issuing from a cloud, and grasping a branch of a rose tree, with four white roses thereon, which touch only the four lowermost Pentacles. No rosebuds even, but only leaves, touch the four uppermost

THE EQUINOX

disks. All the Pentacles are similar to that of the Ace, but without the Maltese cross and wings. They are arranged like the geomantic figure Populus. Above and below them are the symbols ☉ and ♍ for the Decan.

Over-careful in small things at the expense of great: "Penny wise and pound foolish": gain of ready money in small sums; mean; avaricious; industrious; cultivation of land; hoarding, lacking in enterprise.

Hod of ה (Skill: prudence: cunning).

Therein rule those mighty Angels אבאיה and כהתאל.

XXV

THE LORD OF MATERIAL GAIN

Nine of Pentacles

A WHITE Radiating Angelic Hand, holding a rose branch with nine white roses, each of which touches a Pentacle. The Pentacles are arranged thus ⁙ and there are rosebuds on the branches as well as flowers. ♀ and ♍ above and below.

Complete realization of material gain, good, riches; inheritance; covetous; treasuring of goods; and sometimes theft and knavery. The whole according to dignity.

Yesod of ה (Inheritance, much increase of goods).

Herein those mighty Angels הויאל and אלדיה have rule and dominion.

DESCRIPTION OF THE CARDS OF THE TAROT

XXVI
THE LORD OF WEALTH
Ten of Pentacles

AN Angelic Hand, holding by the lower extremity a branch whose roses touch all the Pentacles. No buds, however, are shewn. The symbols of ♉ and ♏ are above and below.

The Pentacles are thus arranged ⁞⁞.

Completion of material gain and fortune; but nothing beyond: as it were, at the very pinnacle of success. Old age, slothfulness; great wealth, yet sometimes loss in part; heaviness; dullness of mind, yet clever and prosperous in money transactions.

Malkuth of ה (Riches and wealth).

Herein are לאיה and ההעיה set over this Decan as Angel Rulers.

XXVII
THE LORD OF PEACE RESTORED
Two of Swords or Pikes

Two crossed swords, like the air dagger of a Z.A.M, each held by a White Radiant Angelic Hand. Upon the point where the two cross is a rose of five petals, emitting white rays. At the top and bottom of the card are two small daggers, supporting respectively the symbol ♎ thus, and ☽ representing the Decanate.

THE EQUINOX

Contradictory characters in the same nature, strength through suffering; pleasure after pain. Sacrifice and trouble, yet strength arising therefrom, symbolized by the position of the rose, as though the pain itself had brought forth beauty. Arrangement, peace restored; truce; truth and untruth; sorrow and sympathy. Aid to the weak; arrangement; justice, unselfishness; also a tendency to repetition of affronts on being pardoned; injury when meaning well; given to petitions; also a want of tact, and asking questions of little moment; talkative.

Chokmah of Vau. Quarrel made up, yet still some tension in relations: actions sometimes selfish, sometimes unselfish.

Herein rule the Great Angels יליאל and מנהאל.

XXVIII

THE LORD OF SORROW

Three of Swords or Spears

THREE White Radiating Angelic Hands, issuing from clouds, and holding three swords upright (as though the central sword had struck apart the two others, which were crossed in the preceding symbol): the central sword cuts asunder the rose of five petals, which in the previous symbol grew at the junction of the swords; its petals are falling, and no white rays issue from it.

Above and below the central sword are the symbols of ♄ and ♑.

DESCRIPTION OF THE CARDS OF THE TAROT

Disruption, interruption, separation, quarrelling; sowing of discord and strife, mischief-making, sorrow and tears; yet mirth in Platonic pleasures; singing, faithfulness in promises, honesty in money transactions, selfish and dissipated, yet sometimes generous: deceitful in words and repetitions; the whole according to dignity.

Binah of ו (Unhappiness, sorrow, and tears).

Herein rule the Great Angels הריאל and הומיה as Lords of the Decan.

XXIX

THE LORD OF REST FROM STRIFE

Four of Swords

Two White Radiating Angelic Hands, each holding two swords; which four cross in the centre. The rose of five petals with white radiations is reinstated on the point of their intersection. Above and below, on the points of two small daggers, are ♎ and ♎, representing the Decanate.

Rest from sorrow; yet after and through it. Peace from and after war. Relaxation of anxiety. Quietness, rest, ease and plenty, yet after struggle. Goods of this life; abundance; modified by dignity as is usual.

Chesed of ו (Convalescence, recovery from sickness; change for the better).

Herein do לאויה and כליאל bear rule.

THE EQUINOX

XXX

THE LORD OF LOSS IN PLEASURE

Five of Cups or Chalices

A WHITE Radiating Angelic Hand, holding lotuses or water-lilies, of which the flowers are falling right and left. Leaves only, and no buds, surmount them. These lotus stems ascend between the cups in the manner of a fountain, but no water flows therefrom; neither is there water in any of the cups, which are somewhat of the shape of the magical instrument of the Zelator Adeptus Minor.

Above and below are the symbols of ♂ and ♏ for the Decan.

Death, or end of pleasure: disappointment, sorrow and loss in those things from which pleasure is expected. Sadness, treachery, deceit; ill-will, detraction; charity and kindness ill requited; all kinds of anxieties and troubles from unsuspected and unexpected sources.

Geburah of ה (Disappointment in love, marriage broken off, unkindness of a friend; loss of friendship).

Herein rule לויה and פהליה.

XXXI

THE LORD OF PLEASURE

Six of Chalices

AN Angelic Hand, as before, holds a group of stems of water-lilies or lotuses, from which six flowers bend, one over

DESCRIPTION OF THE CARDS OF THE TAROT

each cup. From these flowers a white glistening water flows into the cups as from a fountain, but they are not yet full. Above and below are ☉ and ♏ referring to the Decan.

Commencement of steady increase, gain and pleasure; but commencement only. Also affront, detection, knowledge, and in some instances contention and strife arising from unwarranted self-assertion and vanity. Sometimes thankless and presumptuous; sometimes amiable and patient. According to dignity as usual.

Tiphareth of ה (Beginning of wish, happiness, success, or enjoyment).

Therein rule כלכאל and יאל".

XXXII

THE LORD OF ILLUSIONARY SUCCESS

Seven of Chalices

THE seven cups are arranged as two descending triangles above a point: a hand, as usual, holds lotus stems which arise from the central lower cup. The hand is above this cup and below the middle one. With the exception of the central lower cup, each is overhung by a lotus flower, but no water falls from these into any of the cups, which are all quite empty. Above and below are the symbols of the Decanate ♀ and ♏.

Possible victory, but neutralized by the supineness of the person: illusionary success, deception in the moment of apparent victory. Lying, error, promises unfulfilled. Drunkenness, wrath, vanity. Lust, fornication, violence against women,

THE EQUINOX

selfish dissipation, deception in love and friendship. Often success gained, but not followed up. Modified as usual by dignity.

Netzach of ה (Lying, promises unfulfilled; illusion, deception, error; slight success at outset, not retained).

Herein the Angels מלהאל and חהויה rule.

XXXIII

THE LORD OF SWIFTNESS

Eight of Wands or Torches

FOUR White Radiating Angelic Hands (two proceeding from each side) issuant from clouds; clasped in two pairs in the centre with the grip of the First Order. They hold eight wands, crossed four with four. Flames issue from the point of junction. Surmounting the small wands with flames issuing down them, and placed in the centre at the top and bottom of the card respectively, are the symbols of ♂ and ♐ for the Decan.

Too much force applied too suddenly. Very rapid rush, but quickly passed and expended. Violent, but not lasting. Swiftness, rapidity, courage, boldness, confidence, freedom, warfare, violence; love of open air, field-sports, gardens and meadows. Generous, subtle, eloquent, yet somewhat untrustworthy; rapacious, insolent, oppressive. Theft and robbery. According to dignity.

Hod of ' (Hasty communications and messages; swiftness).

Therein rule the Angels כתהיה and האאיה.

DESCRIPTION OF THE CARDS OF THE TAROT

XXXIV
THE LORD OF GREAT STRENGTH
Nine of Wands or Torches

FOUR hands, as in the previous symbol, holding eight wands crossed four and four; but a fifth hand at the foot of the card holds another wand upright, which traverses the point of junction with the others: flames leap herefrom. Above and below are the symbols ♌ and ♐.

Tremendous and steady force that cannot be shaken. Herculean strength, yet sometimes scientifically applied. Great success, but with strife and energy. Victory, preceded by apprehension and fear. Health good, and recovery not in doubt. Generous, questioning and curious; fond of external appearances: intractable, obstinate.

Yesod of ' (Strength, power, health, recovery from sickness).

Herein rule the Angels ירהאל and שאהיה.

XXXV
THE LORD OF OPPRESSION
Ten of Wands

FOUR hands holding eight wands crossed as before. A fifth hand holding two wands upright, which traverses the junction of the others. Flames issuant. ♄ and ♐.

Cruel and overbearing force and energy, but applied only

THE EQUINOX

to material and selfish ends. Sometimes shows failure in a matter, and the opposition too strong to be controlled; arising from the person's too great selfishness at the beginning. Ill-will, levity, lying, malice, slander, envy, obstinacy; swiftness in evil and deceit, if ill dignified. Also generosity, disinterestedness and self-sacrifice, when well dignified.

Malkuth of ו (Cruelty, malice, revenge, injustice).

Therein rule רייאל and אומאל.

XXXVI

THE LORD OF HARMONIOUS CHANGE

Two of Disks or Pentacles

Two wheels, disks or pentacles, similar to that of the Ace. They are united by a green-and-gold serpent, bound about them like a figure of 8. It holds its tail in its mouth. A White Radiant Angelic Hand holds the centre of the whole. No roses enter into this card. Above and below are the symbols of ♃ and ♑. It is a revolving symbol.

The harmony of change, alternation of gain and loss; weakness and strength; everchanging occupation; wandering, discontented with any fixed condition of things; now elated, then melancholy; industrious, yet unreliable; fortunate through prudence of management, yet sometimes unaccountably foolish; alternately talkative and suspicious. Kind, yet wavering and inconsistent. Fortunate in journeying. Argumentative.

Chokmah of ה (Pleasant change, visit to friends).

Herein the Angels לכבאל and ושריה have rule.

DESCRIPTION OF THE CARDS OF THE TAROT

XXXVII
THE LORD OF MATERIAL WORKS
Three of Pentacles

A WHITE-WINGED Angelic Hand, as before, holding a branch of a rose tree, of which two white rosebuds touch and surmount the topmost Pentacle. The Pentacles are arranged in an equilateral triangle. Above and below the symbols ♂ and ♑.

Working and constructive force, building up, creation, erection; realization and increase of material things; gain in commercial transactions, rank; increase of substance, influence, cleverness in business, selfishness. Commencement of matters to be established later. Narrow and prejudiced. Keen in matters of gain; sometimes given to seeking after impossibilities.

Binah of ה (Business, paid employment, commercial transaction).

Herein are יחויה and להחיה Angelic Rulers.

XXXVIII
THE LORD OF EARTHLY POWER
Four of Pentacles

A HAND holding a branch of a rose tree, but without flowers or buds, save that in the centre is one fully blown white rose. Pentacles are disposed as on the points of a square; a rose in its centre. Symbols ☉ and ♑ above and below to represent the Decan.

THE EQUINOX

Assured material gain: success, rank, dominion, earthly power, completed but leading to nothing beyond. Prejudicial, covetous, suspicious, careful and orderly, but discontented. Little enterprise or originality. According to dignity as usual.

Chesed of ה (Gain of money or influence: a present).

Herein do בתיה and מנדאל bear rule.

XXXIX

THE LORD OF DEFEAT

Five of Swords

Two Rayed Angelic Hands each holding two swords nearly upright, but falling apart of each other, right and left of the card. A third hand holds a sword upright in the centre as though it had disunited them. The petals of the rose, which in the Four had been reinstated in the centre, are torn asunder and falling. Above and below are ♀ and ♒ for Decan.

Contest finished and decided against the person; failure, defeat, anxiety, trouble, poverty, avarice, grieving after gain, laborious, unresting; loss and vileness of nature; malicious, slanderous, lying, spiteful and tale-bearing. A busybody and separator of friends, hating to see peace and love between others. Cruel, yet cowardly, thankless and unreliable. Clever and quick in thought and speech. Feelings of pity easily roused, but unenduring.

Geburah of ו (Defeat, loss, malice, spite, slander, evil-speaking).

Herein the Angels אניאל and חעמיה bear rule.

DESCRIPTION OF THE CARDS OF THE TAROT

XL

THE LORD OF EARNED SUCCESS

Six of Swords

Two hands, as before, each holding two swords which cross in the centre. Rose re-established thereon. ♉ and ♒ above and below, supported on the points of two short daggers or swords.

Success after anxiety and trouble; self-esteem, beauty, conceit, but sometimes modesty therewith; dominance, patience, labour, etc.

Tiphareth of ו (Labour, work, journey by water).

Ruled by the Great Angels ההעאל and יואל.

XLI

THE LORD OF UNSTABLE EFFORT

Seven of Swords

Two Angelic Radiating Hands as before, each holding three swords. A third hand holds up a single sword in the centre. The points of all the swords *just touch* each other, the central sword not altogether dividing them.

The Rose of the previous symbols of this suit is held up by the same hand which holds the central sword: as if the victory were at its disposal. Symbols of ♎ and ♒.

Partial success. Yielding when victory is within grasp, as

if the last reserves of strength were used up. Inclination to lose when on the point of gaining, through not continuing the effort. Love of abundance, fascinated by display, given to compliments, affronts and insolences, and to spy upon others. Inclined to betray confidences, not always intentionally. Rather vacillatory and unreliable.

Netzach of ו (Journey by land: in character untrustworthy).

Herein rule the Great Angels ההחאל and מיכאל.

XLII
THE LORD OF ABANDONED SUCCESS
Eight of Chalices

A WHITE Radiating Angelic Hand, holding a group of stems of lotuses or water-lilies. There are only two flowers shown, which bend over the two central cups, pouring into them a a white water which fills them and runs over into the three lowest, which latter are not yet filled. The three uppermost are quite empty. At the top and bottom of the card are symbols ♃ and ♓.

Temporary success, but without further results. Thing thrown aside as soon as gained. Not lasting, even in the matter in hand. Indolence in success. Journeying from place to place. Misery and repining without cause. Seeking after riches. Instability.

Hod of ה (Success abandoned; decline of interest).

The Angels ruling are וליה and ילהיה.

DESCRIPTION OF THE CARDS OF THE TAROT

XLIII
THE LORD OF MATERIAL HAPPINESS
Nine of Chalices

A WHITE Radiant Angelic Hand, issuing from a cloud holding lotus or water-lilies, one flower of which overhangs each cup; from it a white water pours. Cups are arranged in three rows of 3. ♃ and ♓ above and below.

Complete and perfect realization of pleasure and happiness, almost perfect; self-praise, vanity, conceit, much talking of self, yet kind and lovable, and may be self-denying therewith. High-minded, not easily satisfied with small and limited ideas. Apt to be maligned through too much self-assumption. A good and generous, but sometimes foolish nature.

Yesod of ה (Complete success, pleasure and happiness, wishes fulfilled).

Therein rule the Angels סאליה and עריאל.

XLIV
THE LORD OF PERFECTED SUCCESS
Ten of Cups or Chalices

HAND, as usual, holding bunch of water-lilies or lotuses, whose flowers pour a white water into all the cups, which *all run over*. The uppermost cup is held sideways by a hand, and pours water into the left-hand upper cup. A single lotus flower surmounts the top cup, and is the source of the water that fills it. Above and below the symbols ♂ and ♓.

THE EQUINOX

Permanent and lasting success and happiness, because inspired from above. Not so sensual as the "Lord of Material Happiness," yet almost more truly happy. Pleasure, dissipation, debauchery, quietness, peacemaking. Kindness, pity, generosity, wantonness, waste, etc., according to dignity.

Malkuth of ה (Matter settled: complete good fortune).

Herein the Great Angels עשליה and מיהאל rule.

[This is not such a good card as stated. It represents boredom, and quarrelling arising therefrom; disgust springing from too great luxury. In particular it represents drug-habits, the sottish excess of pleasure and the revenge of nature.]

XLV

THE LORD OF DOMINION

Two of Wands

A WHITE Radiating Angelic Hand, issuing from clouds, and grasping two crossed wands. Flames issue from the point of junction. On two small wands above and below, with flames of five issuing therefrom, are the symbols of ♂ and ♈ for the Decan.

Strength, domination, harmony of rule and of justice. Boldness, courage, fierceness, shamelessness, revenge, resolution, generous, proud, sensitive, ambitious, refined, restless, turbulent, sagacious withal, yet unforgiving and obstinate.

Chokmah of י (Influence over others, authority, power, dominion).

Therein the Angels והואל and דביאל bear rule.

DESCRIPTION OF THE CARDS OF THE TAROT

XLVI
THE LORD OF ESTABLISHED STRENGTH
Three of Wands

A WHITE Radiating Angelic Hand, as before, issuing from clouds and grasping three wands in the centre (two crossed, the third upright). Flames issue from the point of junction. Above and below are the symbols ☉ and ♈.

Established force, strength, realization of hope. Completion of labour. Success after struggle. Pride, nobility, wealth, power, conceit. Rude self-assumption and insolence. Generosity, obstinacy, etc.

Binah of ' (Pride, arrogance, self-assertion).
Herein rule the Angels ההשיה and עממיה.
[This card is much better than as described.]

XLVII
THE LORD OF PERFECTED WORK
Four of Wands

Two White Radiating Angelic Hands, as before, issuing from clouds right and left of the card and clasped in the centre with the grip of the First Order, holding four wands or torches crossed. Flames issue from the point of junction. Above and below are two small flaming wands, with the symbols of ♀ and ♈ representing the Decan.

Perfection or completion of a thing built up with trouble

THE EQUINOX

and labour. Rest after labour, subtlety, cleverness, beauty, mirth, success in completion. Reasoning faculty, conclusions drawn from previous knowledge. Unreadiness, unreliable and unsteady through over-anxiety and hurriedness of action. Graceful in manner, at times insincere, etc.

Chesed of י (Settlement, arrangement, completion).

Herein are כבאאל and כיתאל Angelic rulers.

XLVIII
THE LORD OF MATERIAL TROUBLE
Five of Pentacles

A WHITE Radiant Angelic Hand issuing from clouds, and holding a branch of the white rose tree, but from which the roses are falling, and leaving no buds behind. Five Pentacles similar to the Ace. Above and below are א and ח.

Loss of money or position. Trouble about material things. Labour, toil, land cultivation; building, knowledge and acuteness of earthly things, poverty, carefulness, kindness; sometimes money regained after severe toil and labour. Unimaginative, harsh, stern, determined, obstinate.

Geburah of ה (Loss of profession, loss of money, monetary anxiety).

Herein the angels מבהיה and פניאל rule.

DESCRIPTION OF THE CARDS OF THE TAROT

XLIX
THE LORD OF MATERIAL SUCCESS
Six of Pentacles

A WHITE Radiant Angelic Hand holding a rose branch with white roses and buds, each of which touches a Pentacle. Pentacles are arranged in two columns of three each ⋮ ⋮ . Above and below are the symbols ♉ and ☿ of the Decan.

Success and gain in material undertakings. Power, influence, rank, nobility, rule over the people. Fortunate successful, liberal aud just.

If ill dignified, may be purse-proud, insolent from excess, or prodigal.

Tiphareth of ה (Success in material things, prosperity in business).

Herein rule the Angels כמיה and ייאל.

L
THE LORD OF SUCCESS UNFULFILLED
Seven of Pentacles

A WHITE Radiating Angelic Hand issuing from a cloud, and holding a white rose branch. Seven Pentacles arranged like the geomantic figure Rubeus. There are only five buds, which overhang, but do not touch the five uppermost

Pentacles. Above and below are the Decan symbols, ♄ and ♉ respectively.

Promises of success unfulfilled. (Shewn, as it were, by the fact that the rosebuds do not come to anything.) Loss of apparently promising fortune. Hopes deceived and crushed. Disappointment, misery, slavery, necessity and baseness. A cultivator of land, and yet a loser thereby. Sometimes it denotes slight and isolated gains with no fruits resulting therefrom, and of no further account, though seeming to promise well.

Netzach of ה (Unprofitable speculations and employments; little gain for much labour).

Therein הרתאל and מצראל are ruling Angels.

LI

THE LORD OF SHORTENED FORCE

Eight of Swords

FOUR White Radiant Angelic Hands issuing from clouds, each holding two swords, points upwards; all the points touch near the top of the card. Hands issue, two at each bottom angle of the card. The pose of the other sword symbols is re-established in the centre. Above and below are the Decan symbols ♃ and ♊.

Too much force applied to small things: too much attention to detail at the expense of the principal and more important points. When ill dignified, these qualities produce malice, pettiness, and domineering characteristics. Patience

DESCRIPTION OF THE CARDS OF THE TAROT

in detail of study; great care in some things, counterbalanced by equal disorder in others. Impulsive; equally fond of giving or receiving money or presents; generous, clever, acute, selfish and without strong feeling of affection. Admires wisdom, yet applies it to small and unworthy objects.

Hod of ו (Narrow, restricted, petty, a prison).

Therein rule the Angels ומבאל and יההאל.

LII

THE LORD OF DESPAIR AND CRUELTY

Nine of Swords

FOUR Hands, as in the preceding figure, hold eight swords nearly upright, but with the points falling away from each other. A fifth hand holds a ninth sword upright in the centre, as if it had struck them asunder. No rose at all is shewn, as if it were not merely cut asunder, but utterly destroyed. Above and below are the Decan symbols ♂ and ♊.

Despair, cruelty, pitilessness, malice, suffering, want, loss, misery. Burden, oppression, labour, subtlety and craft, dishonesty, lying and slander.

Yet also obedience, faithfulness, patience, unselfishness, etc. According to dignity.

Yesod of ו (Illness, suffering, malice, cruelty, pain).

Therein do עכואל and מהיאל bear rule.

THE EQUINOX

LIII

THE LORD OF RUIN

Ten of Swords

FOUR Hands holding eight swords, as in the preceding symbol; the points falling away from each other. Two hands hold two swords crossed in the centre, as though their junction had disunited the others. No rose, flower or bud, is shewn. Above and below are ☉ and ♊, representing the Decan.

Almost a worse symbol than the Nine of Swords. Undisciplined, warring force, complete disruption and failure. Ruin of all plans and projects. Disdain, insolence and impertinence, yet mirth and jollity therewith. A marplot, loving to overthrow the happiness of others; a repeater of things; given to much unprofitable speech, and of many words. Yet clever, eloquent, etc., according to dignity.

Malkuth of ו (Ruin, death, defeat, disruption).

Herein the Angels רמביה and מכמאל reign.

LIV

THE LORD OF LOVE

Two of Chalices

A WHITE Radiant Hand, issuant from the lower part of the card from a cloud, holds lotuses. A lotus flower rises

DESCRIPTION OF THE CARDS OF THE TAROT

above water, which occupies the lower part of the card rising above the hand. From this flower rises a stem, terminating near the top of the card in another lotus, from which flows a sparkling white water, as from a fountain. Crossed on the stem just beneath are two dolphins, Argent and Or, on to which the water falls, and from which it pours in full streams, like jets of gold and silver, into two cups; which in their turn overflow, flooding the lower part of the card. ♀ and ♋ above and below.

Harmony of masculine and feminine united. Harmony, pleasure, mirth, subtlety: but if ill dignified—folly, dissipation, waste, silly actions.

Chokmah of ה (Marriage, love, pleasure).

Therein rule the Angels אואל and הבויה.

LV

THE LORD OF ABUNDANCE

Three of Chalices

A WHITE Radiating Hand, as before, holds a group of lotuses or water-lilies, from which two flowers rise on either side of, and overhanging the top cup; pouring into it the white water. Flowers in the same way pour white water into the lower cups. All the cups overflow; the topmost into the two others, and these upon the lower part of the card. Cups are arranged in an erect equilateral triangle. ☿ and ♋ above and below.

Abundance, plenty, success, pleasure, sensuality, passive

THE EQUINOX

success, good luck and fortune; love, gladness, kindness, liberality.

Binah of ה (Plenty, hospitality, eating and drinking, pleasure, dancing, new clothes, merriment).

Therein the Angels ראהאל and יבמיה are lords.

LVI

THE LORD OF BLENDED PLEASURE

Four of Chalices

FOUR cups: the two upper overflowing into the two lower, which do not overflow. An Angelic Hand grasps a branch of lotus, from which ascends a stem bearing one flower at the top of the card, from which the white water flows into the two upper cups. From the centre two leaves pass right and left, making, as it were, a cross between the four cups. Above and below are the symbols ♋ and ♌ for the Decan.

Success or pleasure approaching their end. A stationary period in happiness, which may, or may not, continue. It does not mean love and marriage so much as the previous symbol. It is too passive a symbol to represent perfectly complete happiness. Swiftness, hunting and pursuing. Acquisition by contention: injustice sometimes; some drawbacks to pleasure implied.

Chesed of ה (Receiving pleasure or kindness from others, but some discomfort therewith).

Therein rule the great Angels הייאל and מומיה.

DESCRIPTION OF THE CARDS OF THE TAROT

BRIEF MEANING OF TWENTY-TWO KEYS

0. IF the question refers to spiritual matters, the Fool means idea, thought, spirituality, that which endeavours to transcend Earth. But if question is material, it means folly, stupidity, eccentricity, or even mania.

1. Skill, wisdom, adaptation, craft, cunning, or occult wisdom or power.

2. Change, alternation, increase and decrease, fluctuation; whether for good or evil depends on the dignity.

3. Beauty, happiness, pleasure, success. But with very bad dignity it means luxury, dissipation.

4. War, conquest, victory, strife, ambition.

5. Divine wisdom, manifestation, explanation, teaching, occult force voluntarily invoked.

6. Inspiration (passive, mediumistic), motive power, action.

7. Triumph, victory, health (sometimes unstable).

8. Eternal justice. Strength and force, but arrested as in act of judgment. May mean law, trial, etc.

9. Wisdom from on high. Active divine inspiration. Sometimes "unexpected current."

10. Good fortune, happiness (within bounds). Intoxication of success.

11. Courage, strength, fortitude, power passing on to action. Obstinacy.

12. Enforced sacrifice, punishment, loss, fatal and not voluntary, suffering.

13. Time, age, transformation, change involuntary (as

THE EQUINOX

opposed to 18, ✵). Or death, destruction (only latter with special cards). [Specially, a sudden and quite unexpected change.]

14. Combination of forces, realization, action (material effect, good or evil).

15. Materiality, material force, material temptation, obsession.

16. Ambition, fighting, war, courage, or destruction, danger, fall, ruin.

17. Hope, faith, unexpected help. Or dreaminess, deceived hope, etc.

18. Dissatisfaction, voluntary change. Error, lying, falsity, deception. This card is very sensitive to dignity.

19. Glory, gain, riches. With *very* evil cards it means arrogance, display, vanity.

20. Final decision, judgment, sentence, determination of a matter without appeal, *on its plane*.

21. The matter itself. Synthesis, world, kingdom. Usually denotes actual subject of question, and therefore depends entirely on accompanying cards.

[This table is very unsatisfactory. Each card must be most carefully meditated, taking all its correspondences, and a clear idea formed.]

Princes and Queens shew almost always actual men and women connected with the matter.

But the Kings (Knights) sometimes represent coming or going of a matter, according as they face.

The Princesses shew opinions, thoughts, ideas, either in harmony with or opposed to, the subject.

DESCRIPTION OF THE CARDS OF THE TAROT

A Majority of Wands	.	Energy, opposition, quarrel.
,, Cups .	.	Pleasure, merriment.
,, Swords	.	Trouble, sadness, sickness, death.
,, Pentacles	.	Business, money, possessions.
,, Keys .	.	Strong forces beyond the Querent's control.
,, Court Cards .		Society, meetings of many persons.
,, Aces .	.	Strength generally. Aces are always strong cards.
4 Aces	.	Great power and force.
3 Aces	.	Riches, success.
4 Kings (Knights) .		Swiftness, rapidity.
3 ,, ,,	.	Unexpected meetings. Knights, in general, shew news.
4 Queens	.	Authority, influence.
3 Queens	.	Powerful friends.
4 Princes	.	Meetings with the great.
3 Princes	.	Rank and honour.
4 Princesses .	.	New ideas or plans.
3 Princesses .	.	Society of the young.
4 Tens	.	Anxiety, responsibility.
3 Tens	.	Buying and selling (commerce).
4 Nines	.	Added responsibilities.
3 Nines	.	Much correspondence.
4 Eights	.	Much news.
3 Eights	.	Much journeying.

THE EQUINOX

4 Sevens	Disappointments.
3 Sevens	Treaties and compacts.
4 Sixes	Pleasure.
3 Sixes	Gain, success.
4 Fives	Order, regularity.
3 Fives	Quarrels, fights.
4 Fours	Rest, peace.
3 Fours	Industry.
4 Threes	Resolution, determination.
3 Threes	Deceit.
4 Twos	Conferences, conversations.
3 Twos	Reorganization, recommendation.

OF THE DIGNITIES

A CARD is strong or weak, well dignified or ill dignified, according to the cards next to it on either side.

Cards of the same suit on either side strengthen it greatly, for good or evil according to their nature.

Cards of opposite natures on either side weaken it greatly, for either good or evil.

Swords are inimical to Pentacles.

Wands are inimical to Cups.

Swords are friendly with Cups and Wands.

Wands are friendly with Swords and Pentacles.

If a card fall between two others which are mutually contrary, it is not much affected by either.

DESCRIPTION OF THE CARDS OF THE TAROT

A METHOD OF DIVINATION BY THE TAROT

[This method is that given to students of the grade Adept Adeptus Minor in the R. R. et A. C. But it has been revised and improved, while certain safeguards have been introduced in order to make its abuse impossible.—O.M.]

1. THE Significator.

Choose a card to represent the Querent, using your knowledge or judgment of his character rather than dwelling on his physical characteristics.

2. Take the cards in your left hand. In the right hand hold the wand over them, and say: I invoke thee, I A O, that thou wilt send H R U, the great Angel that is set over the operations of this Secret Wisdom, to lay his hand invisibly upon these consecrated cards of art, that thereby we may obtain true knowledge of hidden things, to the glory of thine ineffable Name. Amen.

3. Hand the cards to Querent, and bid him think of the question attentively, and cut.

4. Take the cards as cut, and hold as for dealing.

First Operation

This shows the situation of the Querent at the time when he consults you.

1. The pack being in front of you, cut, and place the top half to the left.

2. Cut each pack again to the left.

3. These four stacks represent I H V H, from right to left.

4. Find the Significator. If it be in the ' pack, the question refers to work, business, etc.; if in the ח pack, to love, marriage, or pleasure; if in the ו pack, to trouble, loss, scandal, quarrelling, etc.; if in the ה pack, to money, goods, and such purely material matters.

5. Tell the Querent what he has come for: if wrong, abandon the divination.

6. If right, spread out the pack containing the Significator, face upwards.

Count the cards from him, in the direction in which he faces.

The counting should include the card from which you count.

For Knights, Queens and Princes, count 4.

For Princesses, count 7.

For Aces, count 11.

For small cards, count according to the number.

For trumps, count 3 for the elemental trumps; 9 for the planetary trumps; 12 for the Zodiacal trumps.

Make a "story" of these cards. This story is that of the beginning of the affair.

7. Pair the cards on either side of the Significator, then those outside them, and so on. Make another "story," which should fill in the details omitted in the first.

8. If this story is not quite accurate, do not be discouraged. Perhaps the Querent himself does not know everything. But the main lines ought to be laid down firmly, with correctness, or the divination should be abandoned.

DESCRIPTION OF THE CARDS OF THE TAROT

Second Operation
Development of the Question

1. Shuffle, invoke suitably, and let Querent cut as before.
2. Deal cards into twelve stacks, for the twelve astrological houses of heaven.
3. Make up your mind in which stack you ought to find the Significator, *e.g.* in the seventh house if the question concerns marriage, and so on.
4. Examine this chosen stack. If the Significator is not there, try some cognate house. On a second failure, abandon the divination.
5. Read the stack, counting and pairing as before.

Third Operation
Further Development of the Question

1. Shuffle, etc., as before.
2. Deal cards into twelve stacks for the twelve signs of the Zodiac.
3. Divine the proper stack and proceed as before.

Fourth Operation
Penultimate Aspects of the Question

1. Shuffle, etc., as before.
2. Find the Significator: set him upon the table; let the thirty-six cards following form a ring round him.

3. Count and pair as before.

[Note that the nature of each Decan is shewn by the small card attributed to it, and by the symbols given in Liber DCCLXXVII, cols. 149–151.]

Fifth Operation

Final Result

1. Shuffle, etc., as before.
2. Deal into ten packs in the form of the Tree of Life.
3. Make up your mind where the Significator should be, as before; but failure does not here necessarily imply that the divination has gone astray.
4. Count and pair as before.

[Note that one cannot tell at what part of the divination the present time occurs. Usually Op. 1 seems to indicate the past history of the question; but not always so. Experience will teach. Sometimes a new current of high help may show the moment of consultation.

I may add that in material matters this method is extremely valuable. I have been able to work out the most complex problems in minute detail. O. M.]

- GOVERNMENT COVER-UPS
- SUPPRESSED SCIENCE
- ALTERNATIVE HEALTH
- UFO'S & THE UNEXPLAINED

ORDER YOUR FREE ISSUE!!

Pay the bill which follows to continue your subscription or keep the issue with no obligation

Call Toll Free:
888 909 7474
NEXUS Magazine 2940 E. Colfax #131, Denver, CO

ORDER FROM YOUR FAVORITE BOOKSELLER OR CALL FOR OUR FREE CATALOG

Of Heaven and Earth: Essays Presented at the First Sitchin Studies Day, edited by Zecharia Sitchin. ISBN 1-885395-17-5 • 164 pages • 5 1/2 x 8 1/2 • trade paper • illustrated • $14.95

God Games: What Do You Do Forever?, by Neil Freer. ISBN 1-885395-39-6 • 312 pages • 6 x 9 • trade paper • $19.95

Space Travelers and the Genesis of the Human Form: Evidence of Intelligent Contact in the Solar System, by Joan d'Arc. ISBN 1-58509-127-8 • 208 pages • 6 x 9 • trade paper • illustrated • $18.95

Humanity's Extraterrestrial Origins: ET Influences on Humankind's Biological and Cultural Evolution, by Dr. Arthur David Horn with Lynette Mallory-Horn. ISBN 3-931652-31-9 • 373 pages • 6 x 9 • trade paper • $17.00

Past Shock: The Origin of Religion and Its Impact on the Human Soul, by Jack Barranger. ISBN 1-885395-08-6 • 126 pages • 6 x 9 • trade paper • illustrated • $12.95

Flying Serpents and Dragons: The Story of Mankind's Reptilian Past, by R.A. Boulay. ISBN 1-885395-38-8 • 276 pages • 6 x 9 • trade paper • illustrated • $19.95

Triumph of the Human Spirit: The Greatest Achievements of the Human Soul and How Its Power Can Change Your Life, by Paul Tice. ISBN 1-885395-57-4 • 295 pages • 6 x 9 • trade paper • illustrated • $19.95

Mysteries Explored: The Search for Human Origins, UFOs, and Religious Beginnings, by Jack Barranger and Paul Tice. ISBN 1-58509-101-4 • 104 pages • 6 x 9 • trade paper • $12.95

Mushrooms and Mankind: The Impact of Mushrooms on Human Consciousness and Religion, by James Arthur. ISBN 1-58509-151-0 • 103 pages • 6 x 9 • trade paper • $12.95

Vril or Vital Magnetism, with an Introduction by Paul Tice. ISBN 1-58509-030-1 • 124 pages • 5 1/2 x 8 1/2 • trade paper • $12.95

The Odic Force: Letters on Od and Magnetism, by Karl von Reichenbach. ISBN 1-58509-001-8 • 192 pages • 6 x 9 • trade paper • $15.95

The New Revelation: The Coming of a New Spiritual Paradigm, by Arthur Conan Doyle. ISBN 1-58509-220-7 • 124 pages • 6 x 9 • trade paper • $12.95

The Astral World: Its Scenes, Dwellers, and Phenomena, by Swami Panchadasi. ISBN 1-58509-071-9 • 104 pages • 6 x 9 • trade paper • $11.95

Reason and Belief: The Impact of Scientific Discovery on Religious and Spiritual Faith, by Sir Oliver Lodge. ISBN 1-58509-226-6 • 180 pages • 6 x 9 • trade paper • $17.95

William Blake: A Biography, by Basil De Selincourt. ISBN 1-58509-225-8 • 384 pages • 6 x 9 • trade paper • $28.95

The Divine Pymander: And Other Writings of Hermes Trismegistus, translated by John D. Chambers. ISBN 1-58509-046-8 • 196 pages • 6 x 9 • trade paper • $16.95

Theosophy and The Secret Doctrine, by Harriet L. Henderson. Includes **H.P. Blavatsky: An Outline of Her Life**, by Herbert Whyte, ISBN 1-58509-075-1 • 132 pages • 6 x 9 • trade paper • $13.95

ORDER FROM YOUR FAVORITE BOOKSELLER OR CALL FOR OUR FREE CATALOG

Babylonian Influence on the Bible and Popular Beliefs: A Comparative Study of Genesis 1.2, by A. Smythe Palmer. ISBN 1-58509-000-X • 124 pages • 6 x 9 • trade paper • $12.95

Biography of Satan: Exposing the Origins of the Devil, by Kersey Graves. ISBN 1-885395-11-6 • 168 pages • 5 1/2 x 8 1/2 • trade paper • $13.95

The Malleus Maleficarum: The Notorious Handbook Once Used to Condemn and Punish "Witches", by Heinrich Kramer and James Sprenger. ISBN 1-58509-098-0 • 332 pages • 6 x 9 • trade paper • $25.95

Crux Ansata: An Indictment of the Roman Catholic Church, by H. G. Wells. ISBN 1-58509-210-X • 160 pages • 6 x 9 • trade paper • $14.95

Emanuel Swedenborg: The Spiritual Columbus, by U.S.E. (William Spear). ISBN 1-58509-096-4 • 208 pages • 6 x 9 • trade paper • $17.95

Dragons and Dragon Lore, by Ernest Ingersoll. ISBN 1-58509-021-2 • 228 pages • 6 x 9 • trade paper • illustrated • $17.95

The Vision of God, by Nicholas of Cusa. ISBN 1-58509-004-2 • 160 pages • 5 x 8 • trade paper • $13.95

The Historical Jesus and the Mythical Christ: Separating Fact From Fiction, by Gerald Massey. ISBN 1-58509-073-5 • 244 pages • 6 x 9 • trade paper • $18.95

Gog and Magog: The Giants in Guildhall; Their Real and Legendary History, with an Account of Other Giants at Home and Abroad, by F.W. Fairholt. ISBN 1-58509-084-0 • 172 pages • 6 x 9 • trade paper • $16.95

The Origin and Evolution of Religion, by Albert Churchward. ISBN 1-58509-078-6 • 504 pages • 6 x 9 • trade paper • $39.95

The Origin of Biblical Traditions, by Albert T. Clay. ISBN 1-58509-065-4 • 220 pages • 5 1/2 x 8 1/2 • trade paper • $17.95

Aryan Sun Myths, by Sarah Elizabeth Titcomb. Introduction by Charles Morris. ISBN 1-58509-069-7 • 192 pages • 6 x 9 • trade paper • $15.95

The Social Record of Christianity, by Joseph McCabe. Includes *The Lies and Fallacies of the Encyclopedia Britannica,* ISBN 1-58509-215-0 • 204 pages • 6 x 9 • trade paper • $14.95

The History of the Christian Religion and Church During the First Three Centuries, by Dr. Augustus Neander. ISBN 1-58509-077-8 • 112 pages • 6 x 9 • trade paper • $12.95

Ancient Symbol Worship: Influence of the Phallic Idea in the Religions of Antiquity, by Hodder M. Westropp and C. Staniland Wake. ISBN 1-58509-048-4 • 120 pages • 6 x 9 • trade paper • illustrated • $12.95

The Gnosis: Or Ancient Wisdom in the Christian Scriptures, by William Kingsland. ISBN 1-58509-047-6 • 232 pages • 6 x 9 • trade paper • $18.95

The Evolution of the Idea of God: An Inquiry into the Origin of Religions, by Grant Allen. ISBN 1-58509-074-3 • 160 pages • 6 x 9 • trade paper • $14.95

Sun Lore of All Ages: A Survey of Solar Mythology, Folklore, Customs, Worship, Festivals, and Superstition, by William Tyler Olcott. ISBN 1-58509-044-1 • 316 pages • 6 x 9 • trade paper • $24.95

Nature Worship: An Account of Phallic Faiths and Practices Ancient and Modern, by the Author of Phallicism with an Introduction by Tedd St. Rain. ISBN 1-58509-049-2 • 112 pages • 6 x 9 • trade paper • illustrated • $12.95

Life and Religion, by Max Muller. ISBN 1-885395-10-8 • 237 pages • 5 1/2 x 8 1/2 • trade paper • $14.95

Jesus: God, Man, or Myth? An Examination of the Evidence, by Herbert Cutner. ISBN 1-58509-072-7 • 304 pages • 6 x 9 • trade paper • $23.95

Pagan and Christian Creeds: Their Origin and Meaning, by Edward Carpenter. ISBN 1-58509-024-7 • 316 pages • 5 1/2 x 8 1/2 • trade paper • $24.95

The Christ Myth: A Study, by Elizabeth Evans. ISBN 1-58509-037-9 • 136 pages • 6 x 9 • trade paper • $13.95

Popery: Foe of the Church and the Republic, by Joseph F. Van Dyke. ISBN 1-58509-058-1 • 336 pages • 6 x 9 • trade paper • illustrated • $25.95

Career of Religious Ideas, by Hudson Tuttle. ISBN 1-58509-066-2 • 172 pages • 5 x 8 • trade paper • $15.95

Buddhist Suttas: Major Scriptural Writings from Early Buddhism, by T.W. Rhys Davids. ISBN 1-58509-079-4 • 376 pages • 6 x 9 • trade paper • $27.95

Early Buddhism, by T. W. Rhys Davids. Includes *Buddhist Ethics: The Way to Salvation?,* by Paul Tice. ISBN 1-58509-076-X • 112 pages • 6 x 9 • trade paper • $12.95

The Fountain-Head of Religion: A Comparative Study of the Principal Religions of the World and a Manifestation of their Common Origin from the Vedas, by Ganga Prasad. ISBN 1-58509-054-9 • 276 pages • 6 x 9 • trade paper • $22.95

India: What Can It Teach Us?, by Max Muller. ISBN 1-58509-064-6 • 284 pages • 5 1/2 x 8 1/2 • trade paper • $22.95

Matrix of Power: How the World has Been Controlled by Powerful People Without Your Knowledge, by Jordan Maxwell. ISBN 1-58509-120-0 • 104 pages • 6 x 9 • trade paper • $12.95

Cyberculture Counterconspiracy: A Steamshovel Web Reader, Volume One, edited by Kenn Thomas. ISBN 1-58509-125-1 • 180 pages • 6 x 9 • trade paper • illustrated • $16.95

Cyberculture Counterconspiracy: A Steamshovel Web Reader, Volume Two, edited by Kenn Thomas. ISBN 1-58509-126-X • 132 pages • 6 x 9 • trade paper • illustrated • $13.95

Oklahoma City Bombing: The Suppressed Truth, by Jon Rappoport. ISBN 1-885395-22-1 • 112 pages • 5 1/2 x 8 1/2 • trade paper • $12.95

The Protocols of the Learned Elders of Zion, by Victor Marsden. ISBN 1-58509-015-3 • 312 pages • 6 x 9 • trade paper • $24.95

Secret Societies and Subversive Movements, by Nesta H. Webster. ISBN 1-58509-092-1 • 432 pages • 6 x 9 • trade paper • $29.95

The Secret Doctrine of the Rosicrucians, by Magus Incognito. ISBN 1-58509-091-3 • 256 pages • 6 x 9 • trade paper • $20.95

The Origin and Evolution of Freemasonry: Connected with the Origin and Evolution of the Human Race, by Albert Churchward. ISBN 1-58509-029-8 • 240 pages • 6 x 9 • trade paper • $18.95

The Lost Key: An Explanation and Application of Masonic Symbols, by Prentiss Tucker. ISBN 1-58509-050-6 • 192 pages • 6 x 9 • trade paper • illustrated • $15.95

The Character, Claims, and Practical Workings of Freemasonry, by Rev. C.G. Finney. ISBN 1-58509-094-8 • 288 pages • 6 x 9 • trade paper • $19.95

The Secret World Government or "The Hidden Hand": The Unrevealed in History, by Maj.-Gen., Count Cherep-Spiridovich. ISBN 1-58509-093-X • 270 pages • 6 x 9 • trade paper • $21.95

The Magus, Book One: A Complete System of Occult Philosophy, by Francis Barrett. ISBN 1-58509-031-X • 200 pages • 6 x 9 • trade paper • illustrated • $16.95

The Magus, Book Two: A Complete System of Occult Philosophy, by Francis Barrett. ISBN 1-58509-032-8 • 220 pages • 6 x 9 • trade paper • illustrated • $17.95

The Magus, Book One and Two: A Complete System of Occult Philosophy, by Francis Barrett. ISBN 1-58509-033-6 • 420 pages • 6 x 9 • trade paper • illustrated • $34.90

The Key of Solomon The King, by S. Liddell MacGregor Mathers. ISBN 1-58509-022-0 • 152 pages • 6 x 9 • trade paper • illustrated • $12.95

Magic and Mystery in Tibet, by Alexandra David-Neel. ISBN 1-58509-097-2 • 352 pages • 6 x 9 • trade paper • $26.95

The Comte de St. Germain, by I. Cooper Oakley. ISBN 1-58509-068-9 • 280 pages • 6 x 9 • trade paper • illustrated • $22.95

Alchemy Rediscovered and Restored, by A. Cockren. ISBN 1-58509-028-X • 156 pages • 5 1/2 x 8 1/2 • trade paper • $13.95

The 6th and 7th Books of Moses, with an Introduction by Paul Tice. ISBN 1-58509-045-X • 188 pages • 6 x 9 • trade paper • illustrated • $16.95

ORDER FROM YOUR FAVORITE BOOKSELLER OR CALL FOR OUR FREE CATALOG

Of Heaven and Earth: Essays Presented at the First Sitchin Studies Day, edited by Zecharia Sitchin. ISBN 1-885395-17-5 • 164 pages • 5 1/2 x 8 1/2 • trade paper • illustrated • $14.95

God Games: What Do You Do Forever?, by Neil Freer. ISBN 1-885395-39-6 • 312 pages • 6 x 9 • trade paper • $19.95

Space Travelers and the Genesis of the Human Form: Evidence of Intelligent Contact in the Solar System, by Joan d'Arc. ISBN 1-58509-127-8 • 208 pages • 6 x 9 • trade paper • illustrated • $18.95

Humanity's Extraterrestrial Origins: ET Influences on Humankind's Biological and Cultural Evolution, by Dr. Arthur David Horn with Lynette Mallory-Horn. ISBN 3-931652-31-9 • 373 pages • 6 x 9 • trade paper • $17.00

Past Shock: The Origin of Religion and Its Impact on the Human Soul, by Jack Barranger. ISBN 1-885395-08-6 • 126 pages • 6 x 9 • trade paper • illustrated • $12.95

Flying Serpents and Dragons: The Story of Mankind's Reptilian Past, by R.A. Boulay. ISBN 1-885395-38-8 • 276 pages • 6 x 9 • trade paper • illustrated • $19.95

Triumph of the Human Spirit: The Greatest Achievements of the Human Soul and How Its Power Can Change Your Life, by Paul Tice. ISBN 1-885395-57-4 • 295 pages • 6 x 9 • trade paper • illustrated • $19.95

Mysteries Explored: The Search for Human Origins, UFOs, and Religious Beginnings, by Jack Barranger and Paul Tice. ISBN 1-58509-101-4 • 104 pages • 6 x 9 • trade paper • $12.95

Mushrooms and Mankind: The Impact of Mushrooms on Human Consciousness and Religion, by James Arthur. ISBN 1-58509-151-0 • 103 pages • 6 x 9 • trade paper • $12.95

Vril or Vital Magnetism, with an Introduction by Paul Tice. ISBN 1-58509-030-1 • 124 pages • 5 1/2 x 8 1/2 • trade paper • $12.95

The Odic Force: Letters on Od and Magnetism, by Karl von Reichenbach. ISBN 1-58509-001-8 • 192 pages • 6 x 9 • trade paper • $15.95

The New Revelation: The Coming of a New Spiritual Paradigm, by Arthur Conan Doyle. ISBN 1-58509-220-7 • 124 pages • 6 x 9 • trade paper • $12.95

The Astral World: Its Scenes, Dwellers, and Phenomena, by Swami Panchadasi. ISBN 1-58509-071-9 • 104 pages • 6 x 9 • trade paper • $11.95

Reason and Belief: The Impact of Scientific Discovery on Religious and Spiritual Faith, by Sir Oliver Lodge. ISBN 1-58509-226-6 • 180 pages • 6 x 9 • trade paper • $17.95

William Blake: A Biography, by Basil De Selincourt. ISBN 1-58509-225-8 • 384 pages • 6 x 9 • trade paper • $28.95

The Divine Pymander: And Other Writings of Hermes Trismegistus, translated by John D. Chambers. ISBN 1-58509-046-8 • 196 pages • 6 x 9 • trade paper • $16.95

Theosophy and The Secret Doctrine, by Harriet L. Henderson. Includes H.P. Blavatsky: An Outline of Her Life, by Herbert Whyte, ISBN 1-58509-075-1 • 132 pages • 6 x 9 • trade paper • $13.95

The Light of Egypt, Volume One: The Science of the Soul and the Stars, by Thomas H. Burgoyne. ISBN 1-58509-051-4 • 320 pages • 6 x 9 • trade paper • illustrated • $24.95

The Light of Egypt, Volume Two: The Science of the Soul and the Stars, by Thomas H. Burgoyne. ISBN 1-58509-052-2 • 224 pages • 6 x 9 • trade paper • illustrated • $17.95

The Jumping Frog and 18 Other Stories: 19 Unforgettable Mark Twain Stories, by Mark Twain. ISBN 1-58509-200-2 • 128 pages • 6 x 9 • trade paper • $12.95

The Devil's Dictionary: A Guidebook for Cynics, by Ambrose Bierce. ISBN 1-58509-016-6 • 144 pages • 6 x 9 • trade paper • $12.95

The Smoky God: Or The Voyage to the Inner World, by Willis George Emerson. ISBN 1-58509-067-0 • 184 pages • 6 x 9 • trade paper • illustrated • $15.95

A Short History of the World, by H.G. Wells. ISBN 1-58509-211-8 • 320 pages • 6 x 9 • trade paper • $24.95

The Voyages and Discoveries of the Companions of Columbus, by Washington Irving. ISBN 1-58509-500-1 • 352 pages • 6 x 9 • hard cover • $39.95

History of Baalbek, by Michel Alouf. ISBN 1-58509-063-8 • 196 pages • 5 x 8 • trade paper • illustrated • $15.95

Ancient Egyptian Masonry: The Building Craft, by Sommers Clarke and R. Engelback. ISBN 1-58509-059-X • 350 pages • 6 x 9 • trade paper • illustrated • $26.95

That Old Time Religion: The Story of Religious Foundations, by Jordan Maxwell and Paul Tice. ISBN 1-58509-100-6 • 103 pages • 6 x 9 • trade paper • $12.95

The Book of Enoch: A Work of Visionary Revelation and Prophecy, Revealing Divine Secrets and Fantastic Information about Creation, Salvation, Heaven and Hell, translated by R. H. Charles. ISBN 1-58509-019-0 • 152 pages • 5 1/2 x 8 1/2 • trade paper • $13.95

The Book of Enoch: Translated from the Editor's Ethiopic Text and Edited with an Enlarged Introduction, Notes and Indexes, Together with a Reprint of the Greek Fragments, edited by R. H. Charles. ISBN 1-58509-080-8 • 448 pages • 6 x 9 • trade paper • $34.95

The Book of the Secrets of Enoch, translated from the Slavonic by W. R. Morfill. Edited, with Introduction and Notes by R. H. Charles. ISBN 1-58509-020-4 • 148 pages • 5 1/2 x 8 1/2 • trade paper • $13.95

Enuma Elish: The Seven Tablets of Creation, Volume One, by L. W. King. ISBN 1-58509-041-7 • 236 pages • 6 x 9 • trade paper • illustrated • $18.95

Enuma Elish: The Seven Tablets of Creation, Volume Two, by L. W. King. ISBN 1-58509-042-5 • 260 pages • 6 x 9 • trade paper • illustrated • $19.95

Enuma Elish, Volumes One and Two: The Seven Tablets of Creation, by L. W. King. Two volumes from above bound as one. ISBN 1-58509-043-3 • 496 pages • 6 x 9 • trade paper • illustrated • $38.90

The Archko Volume: Documents that Claim Proof to the Life, Death, and Resurrection of Christ, by Drs. McIntosh and Twyman. ISBN 1-58509-082-4 • 248 pages • 6 x 9 • trade paper • $20.95

The Lost Language of Symbolism: An Inquiry into the Origin of Certain Letters, Words, Names, Fairy-Tales, Folklore, and Mythologies, by Harold Bayley. ISBN 1-58509-070-0 • 384 pages • 6 x 9 • trade paper • $27.95

The Book of Jasher: A Suppressed Book that was Removed from the Bible, Referred to in Joshua and Second Samuel, translated by Albinus Alcuin (800 AD). ISBN 1-58509-081-6 • 304 pages • 6 x 9 • trade paper • $24.95

The Bible's Most Embarrassing Moments, with an Introduction by Paul Tice. ISBN 1-58509-025-5 • 172 pages • 5 x 8 • trade paper • $14.95

History of the Cross: The Pagan Origin and Idolatrous Adoption and Worship of the Image, by Henry Dana Ward. ISBN 1-58509-056-5 • 104 pages • 6 x 9 • trade paper • illustrated • $11.95

Was Jesus Influenced by Buddhism? A Comparative Study of the Lives and Thoughts of Gautama and Jesus, by Dwight Goddard. ISBN 1-58509-027-1 • 252 pages • 6 x 9 • trade paper • $19.95

History of the Christian Religion to the Year Two Hundred, by Charles B. Waite. ISBN 1-885395-15-9 • 556 pages. • 6 x 9 • hard cover • $25.00

Symbols, Sex, and the Stars, by Ernest Busenbark. ISBN 1-885395-19-1 • 396 pages • 5 1/2 x 8 1/2 • trade paper • $22.95

History of the First Council of Nice: A World's Christian Convention, A.D. 325, by Dean Dudley. ISBN 1-58509-023-9 • 132 pages • 5 1/2 x 8 1/2 • trade paper • $12.95

The World's Sixteen Crucified Saviors, by Kersey Graves. ISBN 1-58509-018-2 • 436 pages • 5 1/2 x 8 1/2 • trade paper • $29.95

ORDER FROM YOUR FAVORITE BOOKSELLER OR CALL FOR OUR FREE CATALOG

Sun Lore of All Ages: A Survey of Solar Mythology, Folklore, Customs, Worship, Festivals, and Superstition, by William Tyler Olcott. ISBN 1-58509-044-1 • 316 pages • 6 x 9 • trade paper • $24.95

Nature Worship: An Account of Phallic Faiths and Practices Ancient and Modern, by the Author of Phallicism with an Introduction by Tedd St. Rain. ISBN 1-58509-049-2 • 112 pages • 6 x 9 • trade paper • illustrated • $12.95

Life and Religion, by Max Muller. ISBN 1-885395-10-8 • 237 pages • 5 1/2 x 8 1/2 • trade paper • $14.95

Jesus: God, Man, or Myth? An Examination of the Evidence, by Herbert Cutner. ISBN 1-58509-072-7 • 304 pages • 6 x 9 • trade paper • $23.95

Pagan and Christian Creeds: Their Origin and Meaning, by Edward Carpenter. ISBN 1-58509-024-7 • 316 pages • 5 1/2 x 8 1/2 • trade paper • $24.95

The Christ Myth: A Study, by Elizabeth Evans. ISBN 1-58509-037-9 • 136 pages • 6 x 9 • trade paper • $13.95

Popery: Foe of the Church and the Republic, by Joseph F. Van Dyke. ISBN 1-58509-058-1 • 336 pages • 6 x 9 • trade paper • illustrated • $25.95

Career of Religious Ideas, by Hudson Tuttle. ISBN 1-58509-066-2 • 172 pages • 5 x 8 • trade paper • $15.95

Buddhist Suttas: Major Scriptural Writings from Early Buddhism, by T.W. Rhys Davids. ISBN 1-58509-079-4 • 376 pages • 6 x 9 • trade paper • $27.95

Early Buddhism, by T. W. Rhys Davids. Includes ***Buddhist Ethics: The Way to Salvation?***, by Paul Tice. ISBN 1-58509-076-X • 112 pages • 6 x 9 • trade paper • $12.95

The Fountain-Head of Religion: A Comparative Study of the Principal Religions of the World and a Manifestation of their Common Origin from the Vedas, by Ganga Prasad. ISBN 1-58509-054-9 • 276 pages • 6 x 9 • trade paper • $22.95

India: What Can It Teach Us?, by Max Muller. ISBN 1-58509-064-6 • 284 pages • 5 1/2 x 8 1/2 • trade paper • $22.95

Matrix of Power: How the World has Been Controlled by Powerful People Without Your Knowledge, by Jordan Maxwell. ISBN 1-58509-120-0 • 104 pages • 6 x 9 • trade paper • $12.95

Cyberculture Counterconspiracy: A Steamshovel Web Reader, Volume One, edited by Kenn Thomas. ISBN 1-58509-125-1 • 180 pages • 6 x 9 • trade paper • illustrated • $16.95

Cyberculture Counterconspiracy: A Steamshovel Web Reader, Volume Two, edited by Kenn Thomas. ISBN 1-58509-126-X • 132 pages • 6 x 9 • trade paper • illustrated • $13.95

Oklahoma City Bombing: The Suppressed Truth, by Jon Rappoport. ISBN 1-885395-22-1 • 112 pages • 5 1/2 x 8 1/2 • trade paper • $12.95

The Protocols of the Learned Elders of Zion, by Victor Marsden. ISBN 1-58509-015-8 • 312 pages • 6 x 9 • trade paper • $24.95

Secret Societies and Subversive Movements, by Nesta H. Webster. ISBN 1-58509-092-1 • 432 pages • 6 x 9 • trade paper • $29.95

The Secret Doctrine of the Rosicrucians, by Magus Incognito. ISBN 1-58509-091-3 • 256 pages • 6 x 9 • trade paper • $20.95

The Origin and Evolution of Freemasonry: Connected with the Origin and Evolution of the Human Race, by Albert Churchward. ISBN 1-58509-029-8 • 240 pages • 6 x 9 • trade paper • $18.95

The Lost Key: An Explanation and Application of Masonic Symbols, by Prentiss Tucker. ISBN 1-58509-050-6 • 192 pages • 6 x 9 • trade paper • illustrated • $15.95

The Character, Claims, and Practical Workings of Freemasonry, by Rev. C.G. Finney. ISBN 1-58509-094-8 • 288 pages • 6 x 9 • trade paper • $22.95

The Secret World Government or "The Hidden Hand": The Unreveraled in History, by Maj.-Gen., Count Cherep-Spiridovich. ISBN 1-58509-093-X • 203 pages • 6 x 9 • trade paper • $17.95

The Magus, Book One: A Complete System of Occult Philosophy, by Francis Barrett. ISBN 1-58509-031-X • 200 pages • 6 x 9 • trade paper • illustrated • $16.95

The Magus, Book Two: A Complete System of Occult Philosophy, by Francis Barrett. ISBN 1-58509-032-8 • 220 pages • 6 x 9 • trade paper • illustrated • $17.95

The Magus, Book One and Two: A Complete System of Occult Philosophy, by Francis Barrett. ISBN 1-58509-033-6 • 420 pages • 6 x 9 • trade paper • illustrated • $34.90

The Key of Solomon The King, by S. Liddell MacGregor Mathers. ISBN 1-58509-022-0 • 152 pages • 6 x 9 • trade paper • illustrated • $12.95

Magic and Mystery in Tibet, by Alexandra David-Neel. ISBN 1-58509-097-2 • 352 pages • 6 x 9 • trade paper • $26.95

The Comte de St. Germain, by I. Cooper Oakley. ISBN 1-58509-068-9 • 280 pages • 6 x 9 • trade paper • illustrated • $22.95

Alchemy Rediscovered and Restored, by A. Cockren. ISBN 1-58509-028-X • 156 pages • 5 1/2 x 8 1/2 • trade paper • $13.95

The 6th and 7th Books of Moses, with an Introduction by Paul Tice. ISBN 1-58509-045-X • 188 pages • 6 x 9 • trade paper • illustrated • $16.95

www.ingramcontent.com/pod-product-compliance
Lightning Source LLC
Chambersburg PA
CBHW070426080426
42450CB00030B/1502